D0556785

UNFUCK AMERICA

UNFUCK AMERICA

A RESPECTFUL, OPEN-MINDED CONVERSATION

★

MIKE RITLAND

UNFUCK AMERICA
A Respectful, Open-Minded Conversation

ISBN   978-1-5445-2486-3   *Hardcover*
       978-1-5445-2488-7   *Paperback*
       978-1-5445-2487-0   *Ebook*

I would like to dedicate this book to...YOU.
Yes, you. If you're picking this up, it
means you give enough of a shit about
this great nation to make it better.

It's also dedicated to all the guests I've had on the
Mike Drop Podcast. If not for them, my take
and perspective on the issues inside this book
would not be as well-rounded and informed.

CONTENTS

★

INTRODUCTION

★

What you hold in your hand isn't just a book. I mean, it is a book; it has pages and binding and a table of contents that lists the topics that will be discussed, which you probably skipped over to get to this part. But this isn't *just* a book. The way I see it, this is the beginning of a conversation—one that you and I both know we need to have.

You don't need me to tell you that a lot is going on in our world right now. Some of it is good. But a large portion of what's happening in our nation is, quite frankly, a shit show. You and I find ourselves living and breathing at a very important and pivotal time in human history. We've come a long way as a species and what we've accomplished over the past several hundred years is nothing short of remarkable. As a nation, the United States has been at the forefront of many of these advancements. It's been an exciting ride on the upward trajectory of technological advancement and evolution.

But as I look at the path ahead, I'm not so sure that we're on track to continue this ascension. Sure, we'll continue to see medical breakthroughs, we'll progress in our use of technology, and we'll continue to optimize every aspect of our human experience. But get on social media for about five minutes or skim just a few of the statistics that are pouring in right now on everything from mental health to drug use to suicide rates to test scores in our nation, and it will become quickly apparent that this little roller coaster we've been so happily riding on is heading for a downward turn—and, if we're not careful, right off the tracks.

If I had to guess, somewhere deep inside, you feel it too. Your ass is starting to pucker up a little bit as you feel that *oh shit* moment that comes just before a roller coaster takes a nosedive. It doesn't take a genius to see the warning signs popping up all around us.

I love this country. I love the principles that it was founded upon. I love the people who live here—the diverse, mixed bag of hardworking, freedom-loving, independent individuals who make up our society. I love this land, from the mountains in Colorado to the wide-open cattle fields in Texas to the sun and waves of Southern California. I was born here, raised here. I offered my life to serve this nation and protect its people. But as I look ahead, I fear for our trajectory. I fear for the future we're creating for the next generation.

And that's why we need to talk.

Because true change will only happen when honest, healthy, and thoughtful conversations take place.

We live in a world inundated with noise. The sound of people shouting their opinions and sharing information from every imaginable outlet—screaming to have their voices heard—surrounds us. We live to the beat of that chaotic symphony, and we've done it for so long we don't even notice the deafening hum that invades every part of our world.

Humans have more methods of communication now than ever before. But though we may be talking, shouting, and cramming information into our minds like a football team with a stack of pizza boxes in front of them, *no one is actually communicating*. No one is sitting down and having real conversations. No one is *really* talking. And we sure as hell aren't listening to each other.

We've become a polarized and divided society that refuses to emerge from our echo chambers to listen to anyone with a differing opinion. We've grown so accustomed to the incessant noise created by biased news outlets, angry people convinced of their own assumptions, and an onslaught of information that we've lost the ability to have any type of substantial, positive conversations with our fellow man. As a result, we miss out on the power that comes from innovative, open minds tackling our world's problems from differing viewpoints and unique perspectives. These honest and thoughtful conversations are what birthed the very government and laws that we built our country upon.

There's a lot of talk these days about wanting these types of conversations to take place, but unfortunately, it rarely happens. That's because you seldom see two people with genuine, mutual respect for one another sit down to talk without a political agenda. You rarely see two people enter a conversation wanting to listen with the goal of truly understanding, rather than convincing the other person of their own position.

And that's a real fucking problem.

In 2018, I launched my podcast, *Mike Drop*, with the primary goal of creating a setting in which authentic, honest conversations like these could take place. I had been a guest on numerous podcasts and was tired of how conversations were so often controlled and restricted. I wanted to sit down with men and women whom I respected and found interesting in an environment where we could take off our professional hats for a few minutes and *just talk* and *listen* to one another.

To create an environment where this could occur, I committed to recording all podcast episodes in person. That means a lot more work logistically, but it is worth it to me to sit eye to eye with people, breathe in the same oxygen, and dispense with stilted conversation and canned Q and A sessions. The simple act of physically being in the same room and looking each other in the eye while recording the podcast is powerful.

Over the years, I've had the opportunity to interview numerous powerful, influential, and incredible people—people like Lara Logan, Andy Stumpf, Nick Irving, Eddie Gallagher, Dakota Meyer, Shawn Ryan, and many more. I didn't bring them on for a labored, manufactured interview. I spent time thinking and preparing myself to have a thoughtful conversation, but we simply looked each other in the whites of our eyes and just talked when we sat down.

No matter who I am sitting across from, I enter each of these conversations with two things at the forefront of my mind. First, I bring a paramount level of respect for the person across from me—respect for who they are, what they've done with their life, and what they bring to the table. That respect also means that I appreciate the fact that they took time out of their busy schedule to sit down with me and talk. Secondly, I come to the table with a genuinely open mind. I'm not strategizing on how to trap them in hard-to-answer questions, not looking to convince them of my point of view, not trying to gain the upper hand in the conversation. I come willing to learn, expand my thinking, shift my perspective, and, yes, even change my mind about something that I thought I knew or understood.

Those two things—a genuine respect for the other person and an open mind—are the primary reasons I believe the *Mike Drop Podcast* has been so successful. As the audience has grown from hundreds to thousands to millions, it has become more and more clear to me just how ravenous our world is for honest conversation.

Through hours of sitting with people from all walks of life, areas of expertise, and positions of power, I have had my mind changed and my perspective challenged. It's expanded my viewpoints and made me a better human being. It made me realize that real change in our world has to begin with individuals having the bravery to speak honestly with others, listen with an open mind, and take responsibility for their own actions and part to play in our world.

And that is the purpose behind this book.

I simply want to have an honest conversation with the other human beings I share this planet with. I want to have a conversation that isn't emotionally or politically charged. I want to throw out some thoughts and ideas, and I want you to throw out yours. If I had it my way, we'd do this over a couple of beers beside my fireplace, but that's obviously not realistic. This book is the next best thing.

So, before we dive in, let's begin where all good conversations should—with respect for one another and an open mind. I don't know a lot about you and your story, but I'd like to share a little of mine, so you have a better idea of who you're talking to and the events that have shaped the thoughts and perspectives I am going to share with you.

I was born in a small town in Iowa and had a simple upbringing. I spent a large portion of my childhood in the great outdoors—running, playing, and swimming. My siblings and I pestered my parents nonstop to get us a dog, and though it took a few years to convince them, I finally got my wish in sixth grade when they surprised all of us with a black Labrador retriever puppy. We thought long and hard on what to name him and landed on Bud. No points for creativity on the name, but we loved him. I couldn't wait to get home from school each day to see him waiting for me—eager and ready to play. I was just a small-town boy with a dog he loved. Little did I realize that my love for dogs would grow into a passion that would shape the course of my life and career.

My obsession with dogs growing up was matched only by my interest in becoming a US Navy SEAL. Both of my grandfathers served in World War II, and from a young age, I had a strong sense of pride for my country and the desire to play an active role in serving and protecting it. As a boy, an article in *Popular Mechanics* about the SEAL teams grabbed my attention, as did the movie *Navy SEALs*, so I set my sights on joining that elite group of individuals.

I joined the navy at seventeen, finished high school, and had to wait until I was eighteen to go through boot camp, which feels like an eternity to an impatient, testosterone-filled teenage boy. I went straight through boot camp and A School and then onto SEAL training. I was officially awarded the trident and was part of my first platoon at SEAL Team 3 by the time I was nineteen. In 2003 I was deployed to Iraq. I saw plenty of action in Operation Iraqi Freedom and had the opportunity to play a role in numerous special operations missions.

It was also in Iraq that I got to witness military working dogs in action. I heard a detailed account of an explosive-detector dog saving Marines' lives by alerting them to a grenade booby trap hidden in a doorway. Upon hearing of this incident, I instantly knew that I wanted to work with similar dogs and utilize their remarkable abilities to defeat the tools of modern warfare. I had grown up around hunting dogs but seeing these incredible creatures perform in combat scenarios captured my attention and piqued my interest. I have always loved dogs, but something just turned on inside of me during my deployment in Iraq. Suddenly, I knew that I wanted to be a part of harnessing the power of these incredible creatures on a much higher level.

From that point forward, I began working with dogs for the remainder of my time in the navy—the last three and a half years of which I also served as a Navy SEAL instructor. I involved myself in all aspects of working with military working dogs, from training to breeding to studying the latest research and science on the subject. At the end of my third enlistment, I decided not to reenlist and instead launched my own dog company, Trikos International, which specializes in providing working K9s to a multitude of clients. Our clients include the Department of Defense (DoD), Department of Homeland Security (DHS), Transportation Security Administration (TSA), US Customs and Border Patrol (CBP), and police departments across the US as well as individuals in need of personal protection dogs.

As business grew rapidly over the years, I was asked to write a couple of different books on the subject—one on special operations working dogs and one on dog training in general. I went for it and jumped into the world of publishing and was humbled and elated when both books hit *The New York Times* Bestsellers list. I was even more pleasantly surprised when my third book, a young adult version of the first, hit the *Times* list as well.

In 2010, I founded the Warrior Dog Foundation, a nonprofit special operations K9 retirement foundation dedicated to serving working military K9s, the special operations community, and their families. I created the foundation to provide a sanctuary for the retirement and rehabilitation of warrior K9s slated for euthanasia. When K9 warriors complete their service, they return home with physical and mental injuries, like many human veterans. Because these special dogs may have a bite history, aggression, and other traits that render them unadoptable, they often receive euthanasia.

I felt that it was wrong to see their lives end in such a way after all they had done to serve our country. The Warrior Dog Foundation helps transition them from an operational environment into a state-of-the-art kennel facility in Texas, ensuring the care of each K9 with dignity and grace, including both mental and physical rehabilitation for the rest of their lives.

After the Warrior Dog Foundation was well established, I developed an online training program for dog owners in 2016 called Trikos Team Dog. Through my time in the dog community, I learned that a lack of training and the resulting behavioral issues were responsible for the surrendering of the majority of shelter dogs. It baffled me to realize that there was such an incredible lack of affordable, readily available resources for dog owners on the market. I had to do something to help, so I combined knowledge from my time as a Navy SEAL multipurpose canine trainer, my experience training Trikos International working dogs, and the techniques developed with the retired working dogs at the Warrior Dog Foundation into a simple training program for everyday dog owners.

As the online training community grew, I also developed and released various dog care and training-related products such as collars, leashes, dog crates, CBD oils, and food and treats. Over the years, I have continued to grow all aspects of the business—from the online training program to the products to the community I've created to support dog owners all across the world.

In 2018, I launched the *Mike Drop Podcast*, which I mentioned above. It has also continued to expand and grow. I have already shared a good bit about my motivation to start the podcast and how that has inspired this book, so I won't go into that again. As the old southern grandmas say, "I don't chew my cabbage twice."

So that's Mike Ritland's life in a nutshell. And now that you have a little bit better of an idea who I am, there are a few things that I want to get clear right off the bat. I'm a straight shooter (no pun intended for all you gun lovers out there), and you'll find out very quickly that I'm direct and to the point. So let's get a couple of things straight.

First of all, I want it said that just because I'm a Navy SEAL doesn't mean that I assume that I know everything, and sure as hell shouldn't lead you to assume that I do either. So don't send me a message asking me questions like, "Does Area 51 exist?" and "Is it true that the government is spraying mind control chemicals on people through crop dusters?" How the fuck would I know? SEALs don't fight aliens. And we probably don't have as much top secret intel as you might think.

I'm proud of what I did and the elite group of individuals I enjoyed serving with. But I'm not naive enough to think that I am better than anyone else or assume that my perspective is more valuable than someone else's simply because I was a SEAL. In some areas, my thoughts and opinions may hold more weight because of the experiences I've had and the skills I've acquired, just like anyone who has dedicated themselves to a particular craft or skill. But I certainly don't want to enter this conversation with you assuming that I think I know everything or have the full picture of all aspects of life. I've put my ego in my back pocket and swallowed my pride, which I believe is a necessary prerequisite for *anyone* who wants to enter into an honest conversation, a conversation which, as we've discussed, requires an ability to have an open mind and pivot if necessary. I forged the thoughts that I will offer in this book through my own journey—one that has been wildly imperfect at times. I have made a shitload of mistakes. I've fallen and gotten back up. I've veered off track and had to course-correct more times than I can count. So while I am confident that I have valuable thoughts and perspectives to offer, I sure as fuck don't think I know everything.

Secondly, I'd like to ask that you not put me in a box or automatically assume to know my thoughts or political leanings just by looking at me without actually listening to what I have to say. It's easy to read about my background and jump to the conclusion that I'm just another alt-right, uberconservative, Donald Trump–loving Republican whose foreign policy basically boils down to sending our military to kick the world's ass whenever possible.

While I hold certain views that would be considered very right-wing or conservative, I also hold many beliefs that would be considered extremely liberal. Some of my thoughts and opinions might surprise you. My belief on almost any social policy would fall in a very liberal category. I am pro-choice, pro–gay marriage, and all for the legalization of drugs. It's not because I personally identify as a homosexual or want my daughters to have an abortion or use drugs myself, but because I believe that the government should leave people the fuck alone in as many areas as possible. Everyone should have the liberty and autonomy to do life as they see fit. So in my view, freedom means giving people the right to marry who they want to marry and smoke what they want to smoke and responsibly own and carry a gun if they want to own and carry a gun. My mantra is pretty simple: *Let me do me, and I'll let you do you, as long as neither involves hurting or harming others.* If it does cause damage to anyone or anything else, you and I should be held fully responsible and accountable for our actions and suffer the consequences of making poor choices.

We'll get into the nitty-gritty details of how this actually translates into politics and laws later, but I ask that you come with an open mind and not place me in a stereotyped box. If you already assume that you know my position before you actually listen to me, this whole honest conversation thing will be headed for the shitter before we even get started. I would never walk up to you, look you up and down, and then pretend to know the intricate thoughts and layered opinions that have formed your beliefs on politics, humanity, and the world at large without getting to know you first. I hope that you will extend that same courtesy to me as well.

Third, I want it said that while I believe that mutual respect between people is absolutely vital, I don't give a shit about your feelings. If you're a listener to the podcast, you already know that line well. I am not here to coddle you, and I'm not here to take care of your emotions. I will not disrespect you, but I have absolutely no regard for your feelings and whether or not they get bruised or rubbed the wrong way.

So check your sensitivities at the door.

If you are ready to be butt-hurt and offended for the sake of being offended, you can go choke yourself. And if that just offended you, I really don't give a shit. And honestly, you should stop giving a shit too. It's a travesty the way we have created a world in which we give over the keys to our internal feelings and emotions to others in the course of a simple conversation. If we're going to have an honest talk, we're not going to get any-where if we spend the whole time doing a fucking ballet dance around each other's feelings. We're all adults here, aren't we? I'm going to tell you right now that, yes, there will be swearing in this book. And if you're the type of asshole who gets offended easily by strong language, then *read this book.* That's right. Not *"don't read this book."* Read this book. If you're offended by my strong language, now is the perfect time for you to practice not giving someone else the power of control over your emotions. Because, let me tell you, the world can be a dangerous place sometimes. So toughen up a bit, mmmmkay?

We're here to dialogue, brainstorm, and strategize about how we can make this nation and the world at large a better place. We're here to figure out how we can roll up our sleeves and fix the problems and challenges we're facing. This isn't Thanksgiving Day with the in-laws where we need to tiptoe around everyone's precious feelings and say *anything* besides what we *really* think.

In the following pages, I'm going to tell you what I think unapologetically, and I'm not going to sugarcoat it. I may say things that hit you the wrong way. It is never my intention to say something simply for the sake of getting a rise out of you, and I will never disrespect you. It's simply my desire to speak my mind and uncover the reality of what is happening in the world around us as honestly as I know how. The truth is sharp, and sometimes it cuts deep. But if the razor's edge of reality stings, it's because the world we live in just hurts sometimes—not because I'm taking cheap shots at you.

Lastly, this is not a one-sided conversation. I invite you to share your thoughts and feedback with me. While I may not respond to every comment, message, or email, I promise that I will truly listen and consider your thoughts and point of view just as you are opening your mind to listen and consider mine.

Let me give you a little overview of how I've structured this book because, if you're like me, it's helpful to have an idea of where we're going and how we're going to get there. I've shaped this book into three major sections, and they are as follows.

We'll start with a reality check about where we are right now as a nation—a collective come-to-Jesus-or-whoever-you-believe-in moment, a look in the proverbial mirror if you will. Spoiler alert: shit's not pretty, folks. But we need to know where we are before we can move forward. We'll also spend some time talking about how we got here and what factors contributed to where we are today. We'll attempt to quiet down the tsunami of political charge, rampant emotion, fake information, and uninformed opinions that seem to surround every important issue of our day. There is so much chaos and noise right now. So much hatred and so many polarizing views. So many people scream rather than listen. We need to take a beat and clear the table. Together, we will remove our blinders and peel back the layers of political biases, emotions, and preconceptions that complicate everything. This is a crucial step before we can move on to discussing the important issues and challenges our country is facing right now.

Then we'll tackle the real shit that needs our attention. We'll discuss border issues, America's inequalities, guns, human trafficking, social issues, the economy, and foreign policy. Within each of these chapters, I will offer my perspectives, beliefs, and thoughts for solutions. I'll also share a framework that I have found personally helpful in assessing these kinds of complicated issues. It's built on *four basic principles*, and it's simple and to the point, just like me.

Additionally, each of these chapters will finish with a conversation about action. About things that you and I, as individuals, can do right now to be a part of changing our country and world for the better. It's not enough for us to have an honest conversation. While it begins there, it must lead to you and me *actually doing something* and taking responsibility for the things within our control. I refuse to allow these pages to simply outline a hundred problems without solutions, to pen a thousand complaints without new ideas. By the end of this book, we will have cleared the chaos, assessed the major issues that we face, and discussed solutions and ideas on the micro level where change really begins.

With me and with you.

So I've laid my cards on the table as clearly and transparently as I know how. In return, I'm going to ask only one thing of you. And that is this:

Listen to understand, not to respond. And if necessary, have the balls to change your mind.

CHAPTER 1

★

AMERICA, THE RICH, SPOILED BRAT

A s Americans, we'd like to think of ourselves as the smartest, wealthiest, freest, best nation in the world. It was only a couple hundred years ago that we, a passionate group of everyday people, rose up and fought to have a country of our own. We had big ideas and ideals. We wanted to see the government conducted in a new way. We wanted to be independent and free. We wanted to be great.

And so, from the time of the Revolutionary War to the period that followed the end of World War II, we put the United States on the map—both figuratively and literally. In the scope of history, a couple hundred years is a mere blip. As a nation, we've accomplished a lot in that short amount of time. We created a new form of government; we built a country founded on independence and freedom. We've grown in power and wealth, and we've made incredible technological advancements. We earned the reputation of being the land of opportunity—respected by the world and regarded as strong, wealthy, and free.

Since the end of World War II and the period just after, we've clutched the coattails of our previous successes and advancements, enjoying the upward swing of the momentum that those before us created. But we haven't done a lot to live up to the standards our predecessors set, and we haven't generated much forward and upward momentum of our own in the past several decades. Sure, we've advanced technology and medicine. We've optimized our lives down to the tiniest details. But as a society, we're falling short. We simply haven't held ourselves to the same standards that those before us set. And it shows. If you aren't sure, don't take my word for it. Sit tight until the end of this chapter because we're going to look at some hard data on this.

The state of our country today can, in many ways, be compared to a chubby, rich, spoiled kid who is born into the fruits of his father's labor. The father worked tirelessly to create a better life than the one he had as a child. His son is born into the product of his blood, sweat, and tears. This success and wealth are his reality from birth; he's never known any different. The son is safe, happy, and well-fed. His needs are provided for him; his life is optimized, easy, and free of care. The father assumes that, with such ample opportunity and resources, the son will soar to greater heights of success and advance further than he had been able to. He can only dream of the greatness that his son will achieve.

But to the father's surprise and disappointment, the son seems preoccupied, easily stressed and exhausted by small things, unwilling to sacrifice comfort in the quest for success. He doesn't strive the way his father did. He isn't accustomed to challenge and hardship. Instead, he's lazy, overfed, complacent, and entitled.

And he's miserable.

The problem is, he is so fucked-up that he doesn't even know he's fucked-up. If you asked him if his family is wealthy, powerful, respected, and safe, he'd answer yes without a second thought. Of course they were. They've always been, haven't they? What the chubby, spoiled, rich kid doesn't realize is that he won't remain wealthy, powerful, respected, and safe by default. Sure, it will appear that way for a time as he enjoys the life his father created, but his way of living has an expiration date. It can't, and it won't, last forever.

The same could be said of America today. Ask anyone if we are the freest, happiest, most powerful nation, and most will answer yes without a second thought. But are we really? Is anyone actually taking a hard look at reality to see if that is still true and if it's going to remain true? Most of us are turning a blind eye like the spoiled brat who throws bills and balance statements in the corner, assuming that the life he's enjoyed will always be there. The problem is that, although he can choose denial for a while, shit will eventually hit the fan, and reality will be a bitch. And the amount of shit hitting that fan will only grow the longer he avoids it.

There is a window of time in which the kid can face reality, clean up his act, get his ass to work, and turn things around. But if he allows that window to pass, he's staring down bankruptcy and the destruction of everything he has been handed.

And that's where we, as a nation, are today.

We are in a window of time when we can still get our act together. We can still take all the resources and opportunity that was hard-earned and worked for that has been handed to us, and we can still reach for greatness. But if that window passes, we risk losing everything. We have to be *proactive* because if we find ourselves in the position of being *reactive*, it's already too late. It's time to take a hard look in the mirror and face reality. As I said, it's not pretty. But if we are willing to face the facts on where we are today and how we got here, we can begin to move forward.

OUR MENTAL HEALTH

On average, there are 132 suicides per day in the United States.

According to the CDC, suicide rates went *up more than 30 percent in half of states since 1999*. What's more, 54 percent of people who died by suicide did **not** *have a known mental health condition.* According to the American Foundation for Suicide Prevention,[1] in 2018 alone, *48,344 people died from suicide.* Suicide is the tenth leading cause of death in the United States.

In 2018, the CDC estimates that 1.4 million suicide attempts took place.[2] It also estimates that in 2015, suicide and self-injury

---

1   "Suicide Statistics." *American Foundation for Suicide Prevention*, December 2, 2020, https://afsp.org/suicide-statistics/.

2   "Suicide Rising across the US," *Centers for Disease Control and Prevention*, June 7, 2018, https://www.cdc.gov/vitalsigns/suicide/index.html.

cost the United States $69 billion. It also surprised me to find out that the rate of suicide is highest in middle-aged White men. White males accounted for 69.67 percent of suicide deaths in 2018, and men died by suicide 3.56 times more often than women.

According to the *Military Times*,[3] the total number of suicides among veterans has increased four of the last five years on record. *From 2007 to 2017, the rate of suicide among veterans jumped almost 50 percent.*

Other mental health issues have skyrocketed as well. According to the CDC,[4] *more than 50 percent of the population will be diagnosed with a mental illness or disorder at some point in their lifetime.* One in five Americans will experience a mental illness in a given year, and one in five children, either currently or at some point during their life, will have a debilitating mental illness.

OUR DRUG ABUSE AND ADDICTIONS

Substance abuse and drug overdose are also at an all-time high. According to the CDC and data from the National Vital Statistics System, there were *70,237 drug overdose deaths* in the United States in 2019.[5] The age-adjusted rate of drug overdose deaths

3   Leo Shane, "New Veteran Suicide Numbers Raise Concerns among Experts Hoping for Positive News." *Military Times*, October 9, 2019, https://www. militarytimes.com/news/pentagon-congress/2019/10/09/new-veteran-suicide-numbers-raise-concerns-among-experts-hoping-for-positive-news/.

4   "Learn about Mental Health—Mental Health—CDC," *Centers for Disease Control and Prevention*, January 26, 2018, https://www.cdc.gov/mentalhealth/learn/index.htm.

5   "Understanding the Epidemic," *Centers for Disease Control and Prevention*,...

increased from 6.1 per 100,000 standard population in 1999 to 21.7 in 2017. The rate increased *by 10 percent per year from 1999 through 2006,* by 3 percent per year from 2006 through 2014, and then *by 16 percent per year from 2014 through 2017.*

According to Addiction Center, *drug overdose deaths have more than tripled* since 1990, and alcohol and drug addiction cost the US economy over $600 billion every year.

The opioid crisis, in particular, is out of control. According to the CDC, from 1999–2018, almost *450,000 people died from an overdose involving any opioid, including prescription and illicit opioids.*[6] The number of drug overdose deaths was *four times higher* in 2018 than in 1999. Since 1999, the sale of opioid painkillers *has skyrocketed by 300 percent.* It's estimated that between 20 and 30 percent of all people who take prescription opioids misuse them, and about 10 percent of people who misuse prescription opioids become addicted to opioids.

According to Addiction Center, about 130 *Americans die every day from an opioid overdose.*[7] From 1999 to 2017, *399,230 Americans lost their lives* to opioids. In 2017 alone, 47,600 fatal overdoses occurred in America, which involved at least one opioid, and doctors issued 191,218,272 opioid prescriptions.

…March 19, 2020, https://www.cdc.gov/drugoverdose/epidemic/index.html.

6   Holly Hedegaard, Arialdi M. Miniño, and Margaret Warner, "Drug Overdose Deaths in the United States, 1999–2017," *NCHS Data Brief,* no. 329 (November 2018), https://www.cdc.gov/nchs/products/databriefs/db329.htm.

7   "Addiction Statistics—Facts on Drug and Alcohol Use," *Addiction Center,* November 24, 2020, https://www.addictioncenter.com/addiction/addiction-statistics/.

And the problem keeps growing. It was estimated 2 million Americans misused prescription opioids *for the first time* in 2017. Approximately 2.1 million Americans have an opioid use disorder. About 5 percent of people with an opioid use disorder will try heroin. The numbers are also staggering for cocaine, methamphetamine, and heroin. I could fill pages with statistics on just the drug problem alone in our nation.

OUR ALCOHOLISM

According to the CDC, excessive alcohol use is responsible for about *one in ten total deaths among working-age adults aged twenty to sixty-four years*.[8] In 2010, excessive alcohol use cost the US economy $249 billion, or $2.05 a drink. About 40 percent of these costs were paid by federal, state, and local governments. The CDC estimates that 37 million US adults—or one in six—binge drink about once a week, consuming an average of seven drinks per binge.[9]

On average, thirty Americans die every day in an alcohol-related car accident, and six Americans die every day from alcohol poisoning.

Approximately 88,000 people die as a result of alcohol every year in the United States.[10]

---

8 "Excessive Alcohol Use." *Centers for Disease Control and Prevention*, September 21, 2020, https://www.cdc.gov/chronicdisease/resources/publications/factsheets/alcohol.htm.

9 Ibid.

10 Ibid.

OUR ADDICTIONS

Gambling and pornography usage have also increased. Gaming revenue for the US commercial casino industry reached an all-time high of $41.7 billion in 2018, up 3.5 percent from the previous year, according to data released today in the American Gaming Association's (AGA) "State of the States 2019: The AGA Survey of the Commercial Casino Industry."[11]

The famed explicit site Pornhub recently stated that its site received over 30 billion hits in 2018. Of those hits, the United States was the biggest consumer. Americans stayed on the site longer than any other nationality, and their time spent viewing porn increased from the previous year.[12]

We're also facing another type of addiction that we've never seen before. And that is technology addiction. According to the CDC, kids aged eight to eighteen now spend, on average, a *whopping seven and a half hours in front of a screen for entertainment each day*, four and a half of which are spent watching TV.[13] Over a year, that adds up to 114 *full days watching a screen for fun*. And

---

11 "Commercial Casino Gaming Revenue Reaches $41.7 Billion in 2018, an All-Time High." *American Gaming Association*, June 11, 2019, https://www.prnewswire.com/news-releases/commercial-casino-gaming-revenue-reaches-41-7-billion-in-2018--an-all-time-high-300865020.html.

12 Manny Alvarez, "Porn Addiction: Why Americans Are in More Danger than Ever." *Fox News Network*, January 16, 2019, https://www.foxnews.com/health/porn-addiction-why-americans-are-in-more-danger-than-ever.

13 "Screen Time vs. Lean Time," *Centers for Disease Control and Prevention*, January 29, 2018, https://www.cdc.gov/nccdphp/dnpao/multimedia/infographics/getmoving.html#:~:text=According%20to%20the%20Kaiser%20Family,watching%20a%20screen%20for%20fun.

that's just the time they spend in front of a screen for entertainment. It doesn't include the time they spend on the computer at school for educational purposes or at home for homework.

And parents aren't much better. *Many adults spend in excess of twelve hours per day in front of a screen of some kind.* Some research shows that the top 20 percent of smartphone users have daily screen time in excess of four and a half hours. A recent Deloitte survey found the average American checks their phone forty-seven times a day.[14]

OUR PHYSICAL HEALTH

Obesity, heart disease, and nutrition-based issues are also out of control. According to the CDC, the prevalence of obesity was 42.4 percent in 2017–2018.[15] From 1999 through 2018, *the prevalence of obesity increased from 30.5 percent to 42.4 percent,* and the prevalence of severe obesity increased from 4.7 percent to 9.2 percent.

Obesity-related conditions include heart disease, stroke, type 2 diabetes, and certain types of cancer that are some of the leading causes of preventable, premature death. *The estimated annual medical cost of obesity in the United States was $147 billion*

14 "Device Addiction Shift to Device Etiquette," Deloitte Development, 2017, https://www2.deloitte.com/content/dam/Deloitte/us/Documents/technology-media-telecommunications/us-tmt-global-mobile-consumer-survey-2017-infographic.pdf.

15 "Heart Disease Facts." *Centers for Disease Control and Prevention,* September 8, 2020, https://www.cdc.gov/heartdisease/facts.htm.

in 2008; the medical cost for people who have obesity was $1,429 higher than those of average weight.

The prevalence of childhood obesity was 18.5 percent and affected about 13.7 million children and adolescents.[16]

And it's not just obesity. According to the CDC, *one person dies every thirty-seven seconds in the United States from cardio-vascular disease.*[17] *About 647,000 Americans die from heart disease each year—that's one in every four deaths.* Heart disease cost the United States about $219 billion each year from 2014 to 2015. This includes the cost of healthcare services, medicines, and lost productivity due to death.

OUR EDUCATION SYSTEM

The United States' education systems also continue to suffer, and our rankings worldwide are just plain embarrassing when you look at the high school graduates we're producing versus the rest of the world. According to World Population Review, "Despite the United States having the second-best education system in the world, it consistently scores lower than many other countries in benchmarks such as math and science and its education ranking was thirty-eighth in math scores and twenty-fourth in science. The United States' education rankings have been falling by international standards over the past three decades, as

---

16 "Childhood Obesity Facts," *Centers for Disease Control and Prevention*, June 24, 2019, https://www.cdc.gov/obesity/data/childhood.html.

17 "Heart Disease Facts." *Centers for Disease Control and Prevention*, September 8, 2020, https://www.cdc.gov/heartdisease/facts.htm.

the government has decreased education funding by 3 percent. Other countries have increased their education funding."[18]

So don't say I didn't warn you—because I did. The truth isn't pretty right now. If statistics like this don't alarm you, I don't know what would. You'd think that with all the natural resources we've been given, the freedoms we enjoy compared to the rest of the world, and the opportunities we are afforded that we'd be soaring. You'd think we'd be happier, healthier, and wealthier than ever.

But we are quite literally killing ourselves.

We are the chubby, entitled rich kid who spends his days eating, drinking, surfing porn, and popping pills. This can't be the world we hand to our children. This can't be the mark we leave on history.

But despite how unsettling these facts are, *this isn't even the scariest part.*

The scary part is that surrounding each of these issues is a minefield of polarizing political views, biased media, and mobs of people shouting so loud that no one can hear a damn thing. Every issue I've shed light on above is caught in a battlefield of opposing views. Our country can't agree on a solution for a single one of those issues. *Everything is politicized right now.* The average person feels the undercurrent of agenda and the pressure to pick sides on things that should never have become a

---

18 "Education Rankings by Country 2020," World Population Review, last accessed December, 2020, https://worldpopulationreview.com/country-rankings/education-rankings-by-country.

battle in the first place. We are so busy screaming out our own beliefs and opinions, so busy choosing sides and stupidly spouting off the party line and position without thinking for ourselves, that nothing can be accomplished.

What's more, our society has become so incredibly divided and polarized that we live in a time where we *hate* those with conflicting beliefs. We lack basic human empathy for those who do not share our perspectives and values. We are so convinced of our own positions, so accustomed to our echo chambers of like minds, that we are incredulous that anyone could disagree with us, and we feel justified to hate and wish them harm when they do.

We celebrate the demise of those with differing stances. We laugh and jeer when personal information is exploited on our tabloids as long as it is at the expense of "the other side." We celebrate the crumbling and total destruction of professional and political careers. We have even grown alarmingly more comfortable with violence and wrongful imprisonment—turning a blind eye and not giving a fuck as long as it's not one of "our people."

We have removed all human association with "the other side." We look at those who politically disagree with us as the enemy. When did it become okay to hate our fellow countrymen simply because of differing opinions?

This should be the thing that alarms us the most.

People often ask how it was possible for the Holocaust to take place. One man cannot pull off an atrocity of that magnitude by himself. How did Hitler convince thousands of people to follow him? How could people be motivated to round up their fellow men, throw them into cattle cars, herd them into gas chambers, and smile as they shoved their bones into the earth?

The answer lies in the fact that it didn't happen overnight. It happened over a period of time as media and strategic propaganda made every aspect of life politicized and pushed people into becoming polarized. As people were forced to take sides, the gap between them widened and widened until *each side could look across the divide and no longer see humans, only enemies.*

We aren't there yet. But don't be naive enough to think that it couldn't happen if we don't make a change. I think the turmoil created by the summer 2020 riots on one side and the storming of the Capitol building during Biden's electoral certification on the other shows just how goddamn dangerously close we are to exactly that. The greatest threat to our society does not lurk out in the distance or across some ocean. It lies right within our borders.

We have become our own worst enemy.

In the following chapters, we will discuss the contributing factors that led us to the place that we find ourselves in today— sad, angry, offended, addicted, and hateful. It is vastly important that we recognize the patterns and elements in our society that brought us to where we are now. It's the only way we will ever be able to remove our blinders and biases, lay down our swords, shut up, and actually move forward toward the betterment of our society.

CHAPTER 2

★

HOW'D WE GET SO FUCKED ANYWAY?

t's fairly obvious after reading through the dismal statistics from the last chapter that America is growing weaker, sicker, and feebler with each passing year. Threads of addiction, overdependence, sensitivity, and sickness have become part of our very fabric. As a nation, we have created the most vulnerable, unprepared, and defenseless society that we have ever had in terms of preparedness to care for ourselves without total dependency on outside help. We are also easily the most sensitive and emotional generation in our nation's history, which is something we'll take a deeper look at in the chapters to come.

When did we become so anemic and easily offended? When did we become so sickly, reliant, and emotionally delicate?

What caused the weakening of our country? How'd we get so fucked anyway?

I believe there are several factors at play.

OVERCORRECTION AND THE EXULTATION OF VICTIMHOOD

They say the road to hell is paved with good intentions. And that couldn't be truer. After the years of struggle our nation faced with the Great Depression, followed by years at war, our nation enjoyed a time of peace and a massive economic boom. During this time, we turned inward and assessed and confronted battles within our own society. We took a good look around and realized that there were groups of people who had been mistreated, and we set out to make changes and do something about it. The fight for rights and equality between races, genders, and sexual orientations were among the issues at the very forefront of those battles.

During that time, a lot of necessary and good changes took place. Injustice was exposed. Laws were passed. Mindsets began to shift. Measures were put into place to level the playing field and bring a sense of fairness to every individual—ensuring that the cards were not stacked in one person's favor over another.

This was accomplished by people with good hearts and the best intentions, many of whom brought about needed change in our society. But, as more light was shed on how minority groups had been mistreated in the past, society became more and more zealous in attempting to right past wrongs and make amends. And, as is true in most areas of life, when change takes place, the propensity toward overcorrection is almost unavoidable. This has led to many elements of overcompensation because the guilt and empathy for past wrongdoings have made these overcorrections appear good and right, fair even, after all that had taken place.

As time moved on, the fight for basic equality evolved into something else. After a while, it wasn't just about legalizing gay marriage, giving women the right to vote, or removing oppressive laws that targeted people of color anymore. It moved into putting measures into place such as affirmative action and mandatory diversity hires. At first glance, it seemed that our nation was simply continuing to level the playing field by providing all people with equal opportunities, but the quest for creating *equal opportunity* morphed into a crusade for creating *equal outcome*.

And many people began to see those as one and the same.

This only increased the need for more measures, more special accommodations. And over time, that level playing field developed a new imbalance. Suddenly, being in a minority group actually had the potential to open up opportunities. Opportunities in education, business, or even to simply be seen and heard. Through this process, our society began to spotlight and exult anyone who has been victimized. And what once might have been a setback or the cause of unfair treatment is now a cause for special accommodations.

An essay centering around a story of victimization in some form or fashion probably ensures a greater chance of getting into a college than a story of accomplishment in this day and time. In our current climate, being a woman, a person of color, or of homosexual orientation might actually open *more* opportunities for climbing the corporate ladder than not. Our country exults the victim; it prizes the one with more disadvantages. This shift in thinking is where a dark side to this righteous quest began.

Now, we have a culture in which people look around, and when they don't see their lives having the same outcome as someone else's, they assume it's due to injustice. This need to create a fair outcome has become prevalent in modern parenting practices and has woven its way into our school systems. Boundaries are not upheld, and kids are constantly deprived of the growth opportunity that failure, consequence, and struggle provides. Additionally, victimhood mentality is often passed down from parent to child as well, raising a generation of entitled adults.

And while there are certainly those who leaped at the chance for a fair opportunity and shed all identity of being victimized as quickly as possible, others seemed to do the opposite. Many seem to run towards it. And now we have a competition for who has been victimized the most or experienced the most setbacks.

This emphasis only causes people to spend time focusing on their perceived lacks, offenses, and disadvantages. Nothing will make society weaker than its members getting into a competition to see who has it worse or who has been victimized the most. Nothing weakens motivation toward achievement like despising those who appear strong, successful, or well-equipped for life.

The more special accommodations are put into place, the more we teeter toward a socialistic society where the government divides up equal slices of pie to each person, irrespective of their work to earn it. This undermines the very foundation of our nation's identity as the land of *opportunity*. Equal opportunity gives everyone a fair shot; it allows you to enter a level playing field and give it your all—to bleed, sweat, and earn your success. However, if we are the land of giving-a-hundred-special-rules-for-a-hundred-special-cases and the land of trying-to-create-an-equal-outcome, you will see a society lose its fire, passion, and ambition.

The game is no longer about trying to stack the odds in your favor but rather competing for how many ways they can be stacked against you. This has a powerful and weakening effect on society at large.

Additionally, I believe that many of the recent measures put in place to help those who we perceive to be at a disadvantage only reinforce the very thing we set out to abolish in the first place—that people should be treated differently because of their gender, race, or sexual orientation. Every time we cross the line and go from simply creating equal *opportunity* to actually trying to create *equal outcomes*, we perpetuate the mentality that "they," whoever that is, can't enter a level playing field and accomplish success on their own.

Here in the South, you'll often hear cute little southern grandmas say, "Oh bless your little heart," in response to hearing of someone's hardship. While said innocently enough and not all that offensive coming out of a seventy-year-old woman with a pie in her hand, there's an unmistakable element of condescension.

"You poor little thing, bless your heart. I pity you. Must be so hard to be you."

It sets one person above another, making the receiver of the words feel small. In the same way, that's what affirmative action and diversity hiring does. It perpetuates the idea that a group of individuals can't achieve success on their own. It's demeaning. It's disrespectful. And in the end, it will actually be the thing that grows and deepens the very problem we set out to solve.

Which is worse, to get out on the field and play your heart out but come up short or to play, win, and then suddenly look around and realize that all the other players conspired to give you special advantages because they didn't think you were equipped to play on their level?

I think we'd all answer the question the same way.

Denying anyone the opportunity to achieve success based solely on their own merit is the greatest injustice of all.

Through this process, people have become conditioned to assume that it is the government's job to ensure that its citizens are provided with an *equal outcome.* You have a sheltered, naive generation that has reached adulthood with the idea that the government is not simply there to protect our abilities in the *pursuit of happiness* but rather that the government is there to *guarantee our happiness.* It is not the government's job to ensure that we are healthy, wealthy, or happy. It is simply to protect our rights so that we have the *ability* to make ourselves any of those things.

This quest, to not only allow every person an equal shot at playing the game but also rigging it so that everyone who plays it is a winner, has created a society that is constantly looking for some external source to create success rather than looking internally and getting shit done on an individual level.

Thus the predicament that we find ourselves in now—our society expects the government to legislate happiness and success and is willing to give up their freedom in exchange for someone else doing the work for them.

In the words of Benjamin Franklin, "Those who would give up essential Liberty, to purchase a little temporary Safety, deserve neither Liberty nor Safety."

That statement is so simple yet brilliantly profound. Prison could be considered one of the "safest" places on Earth. It's a solid and secure structure, eliminating danger from the outside elements and threats, is it not? But in reality, it's one of the most dangerous places on Earth because of its inhabitants. Far too many people are willing to accept a prisoner's mentality and hand over their freedom in lieu of the prospect that the government will keep them safe and guarantee their success and happiness.

The irony is that many of the most outspoken people about wanting to motherfuck the government because of the ways they have been "mistreated" are the very ones who want the government to regulate and legislate everything from happiness to good behavior.

No matter your political leanings or which party you belong to—left, right, Republican, Democrat, Libertarian, or Transhumanist—it should be all of our desire to have the government be as limited as possible, existing only to protect its citizens' ability to make themselves successful should they choose to do so.

I'm all for creating equal opportunity. I'm in favor of leveling the playing field. However, I believe that the overcorrections we have made, and the exaltation of victimhood that we have created as a result, have played a pivotal role in weakening our country.

THE DOWNSIDE OF HUMAN ADVANCEMENT

"Hard times create strong men. Strong men create good times. Good times create weak men. And, weak men create hard times."
—G. Michael Hopf

After World War I, our country was quickly thrown into the Great Depression, then World War II, followed by the Korean War. Our country spent the better part of two and a half decades struggling and fighting for survival, protecting our way of life. We were presented with circumstances that were hard and challenges that no one wanted to face.

But we faced them anyway. We took the struggles, battles, and challenges head-on, and we came out on top. And in the years that followed, we saw one of the greatest economic booms that our nation has ever seen. To use the quote above, those hard times created a strong generation, and that strong generation created good times. But those good times have created a weak generation, and we're on the brink of that weak generation creating hard times again. This goes back to the analogy of the spoiled rich kid discussed in the previous chapter. We have become so comfortable that we've become complacent.

The need for struggle, to fight to survive, is integral to our humanity. Nobody *likes* to struggle, but it is the most effective catalyst in promoting growth. Take a look at nature, and you'll see that struggle is a necessary component of survival. On some level, we all crave it.

In the aftermath of the greatest century of technological advancement the world has ever seen, we find ourselves in a happy, cushioned bubble—free from the majority of the struggles that every human in all previous times in history faced. Incredible improvements have occurred in food, medicine, mechanics, and technology. And for the first time in world history, humans find themselves in a time where they no longer have to worry about putting food on the table or dying of simple, curable diseases. Our lives are filled with relative ease, comfort, and convenience—free from the daily struggle to survive.

And while few people have the desire to return to the way things were before, it's important to face the fact that we have created an entirely new way of living, and some downsides come along with it. This absence of struggle means that we also miss out on the resulting growth. For most people, that primal fight or fire has become sedated and lethargic. For others, it is grossly misguided and shows up in all kinds of unhealthy ways.

A few people seek challenge and relish the opportunity to struggle and fight to succeed. You see this exhibited in the rise of extreme sports in our culture. You see individuals choosing to pursue a demanding career. You also see this shown in people's eagerness to join in any political fight or battle against injustice. This small percentage of the population searches for struggle in the face of ease because it makes them feel alive.

But that's not the case for most. More often than not, humans will choose the path of least resistance, the state of ease and safety. They will choose compliance and complacency rather than freedom and struggle. When given a choice, most people will take the path they perceive to be the easiest. And our world has made it far too easy to drift without direction, sedated by the comforts of our society—reminiscent of the human blobs in the *Matrix* series of movies.

We are supposed to be the strongest and smartest species on the planet, and yet, ironically, our own advancement could also be the cause of our demise if we aren't careful. Our lives are convenient, comfortable, and easy. If you're hungry, food is plentiful. If you need to get somewhere, transportation is available. If you want to communicate with someone, you only have to tap your fingers and you're connected. If you want to lose weight, there are pills and surgery for it. If you don't like the way you are feeling, some substances can alter it.

When faced with the decision to either endure hardship head-on and allow it to make them stronger or to circumvent the struggle altogether, most people will choose the latter. It's easier to snort a little white pile of drugs than it is to face your inner demons. It's easier to go to a doctor and ask for a pill than to eat healthier. It's easier to let the media and politicians dictate how you think, feel, and vote than to go do the work to be a thoughtful and informed individual. It's easier to sit in a La-Z-Boy binging your favorite Netflix series than to get off your ass and work out.

I believe this is the reason that addiction is so rampant right now. Addiction is a perfect deflection tactic. It gives people the ability to completely disconnect from their problems or the gnawing feeling that they need to change or take action in their lives. Even if this escapism is achieved through means that have compounding negative effects, many still find it to be the easier, preferable option over facing reality, taking responsibility, and moving to action. It doesn't help that humans now have a buffet of options—a build-your-own omelet of choices available to numb, sidestep, and bypass struggle.

I see this especially true in the world of health, medicine, and pharmaceuticals. We've created a quick fix for pretty much every ailment and human discomfort under the sun. In doing so, we've bypassed many of our body's warning signs, signals that tell us that we need to change something. If we aren't sleeping, we want a pill. If we are overweight, we want a pill. If our blood pressure is high, we want a pill. We have become grossly overmedicated in our quest to manage symptoms while turning a blind eye to the cause. In our arrogance, we've come to assume that humanity, with its inventions and advancements, is smarter than Mother Nature. And we're not.

Yes, we've done some pretty amazing things and had some very remarkable and commendable breakthroughs medically. But we've severed the connection between cause and effect in our lives. We've lost the motivation to make difficult choices for the greater good because massive industries and businesses are devoted to enticing us with an easier choice. Pop a pill, go through a drivethrough, stay cozy, pick up your remote, and press *play next episode*.

However, we are missing out on the opportunity to become stronger and more resilient at every turn. There is no substitute for discipline, consistency, and hard work. And while the advancements that we have made are amazing, this pursuit and attachment to ease has also made us weaker.

CELEBRITY POLITICIANS AND THE
POLARIZATION OF POLITICAL PARTIES

The other major component in the weakening of our country concerns a shift in politics. In the previous chapter, I touched briefly on the dangers of polarized political parties, but I believe it's worth diving into a little more here.

A split in political perspective and the resulting development of political parties dates back to the very beginning of our nation. During the struggle over ratification of the federal Constitution of 1787, political factions or parties began to form as two differing views emerged on the role of government. Friction between them heightened as attention shifted from creating a new federal government to the question of how powerful that federal government would be. At that time, the two political parties consisted of the Federalists, who wanted a strong central government, and the Anti-Federalists, who advocated for states' rights instead of centralized power. The ensuing partisan battles led George Washington to issue a warning in his farewell address as president of the United States, saying, "Let me now take a more comprehensive view, and warn you in the most solemn manner against the baneful effects of the spirit of party generally."

If only we had listened.

To have a balanced political environment, it is important to have differing views represented well. Robust discussion, passionate conviction, and even voiced disagreement are all part of having a healthy democracy. For most of our nation's history, a general respect was maintained between those who disagreed with each other, even though there were differences in parties and beliefs. The individuals who took part in political discussions were typically ones who invested a good deal of time thinking, researching, and studying government and politics. These discussions weren't void of feeling or passion. They were fueled by the strong convictions of thoughtful individuals, which, at times, meant a display of fiery disagreement and lively debate. But there was still an element of dignity and mutual respect between people.

Over the past handful of decades, all that has changed.

Political parties no longer simply serve as an embodiment of differing viewpoints. They have become a social club or "team" with which to belong. Our political climate has become more about people sitting in bleachers, holding signs, and blindly cheering for their guy to win while lobbing insults at the other side rather than pursuing the betterment of society and the stimulation of thoughtful discussion around relevant issues.

This dynamic has also led to the celebritization of our politicians. Politicians are no longer men and women of conviction with a desire to represent and serve their constituents well. They have become full-blown celebrities—hyping crowds of cheering people and giving out autographs like rock stars. Their crowds cackle and jeer as they sling personal insults and mock the opposition.

There is a disturbing level of blind loyalty to one's party and an automatic, adopted hatred for the other as a result. Gone are the days of respectful, thoughtful discussions. Even basic human respect is rarely shown. Everyone is so consumed by the game of it all—the smearing of the other side and the winning—that we've forgotten that the point is to protect and promote a free and peaceful society.

It has become a Crips versus Bloods mentality. Each group is willing to do things that are detrimental to themselves and their children's future if it hurts the other side. They are blinded by their allegiance to their gang, deviating only if it serves themselves individually. Not only is there disagreement between political parties, but neither side can even fathom or respect any person with an opinion that differs from their own. Sweeping generalizations are made, and stereotypes are slapped on the opposition like cheap stickers at a garage sale.

Democrats think all Republicans are gun-toting, beef-eating, tobacco-spitting, ignorant, redneck, Bible-thumping country-folk who want to blast the world with nukes and don't give a fuck about anything but getting rich and screwing over everyone else. Republicans think Democrats are soy-latte-sipping, superelitist, tree-hugging, arrogant, ultraliberal asshole activists who want to create a socialistic government and think that their shit doesn't stink.

You may snicker at my description, but unfortunately, this personifies what most people think of the other side. What's more, people assume that if you check one box in alignment with a certain party, you must check them all. People assume that if you support the military that you must be a down-the-line, fiery, racist Republican. Or if you support gay rights, you are a hyperliberal socialist.

It's ridiculous and reveals how little we actually assume that people are thinking for themselves. We have generalized and polarized our parties. Both sides say the other is stupid and uninformed. Both say the other side is filled with deceit and corruption. Both accuse the other side of things that they are completely unwilling to address within their own party. The stench of hypocrisy is unbelievable. There is no respect in discussion and no appreciation for a differing viewpoint or the human behind it.

The polarization of political parties and this gang-like allegiance to them has turned far too many people into blind supporters who follow their leader like a flock of fucking sheep. People no longer think for themselves or ask questions. Most scan a couple of social media headlines and hear a few sound bites and call themselves informed—spouting the party line and rattling off their opinions without any real knowledge of the issues at hand.

People are so filled with hatred for the other side that they will vote against any opposing candidate, no matter what corruption is unearthed *in their own* candidate. Case in point: during the 2020 election, Democrats went on record saying that Joe Biden could boil babies and eat them, and they would still vote for him because of how much they hate Donald Trump. And vice versa.

It's a total shit show.

To add to this, money and all its seductive allure is now intertwined with politics in a way that our forefathers probably never expected. Backdoor deals and handshakes are par for the course. Politicians often quadruple their net worth by the time they leave office, if not multiplying it by much more. Can you imagine the looks on the faces of the Founding Fathers if we told them how much money it takes to run a successful campaign these days? It's staggering and deeply troubling.

How can we, as citizens, expect to be properly represented and our interest protected in this environment? How can we expect corruption *not* to take place? Why are we surprised that the majority of the people in politics are power-hungry vultures? Unfortunately, there is no great solution to fix this problem. The problem lies with our lawmakers and enforcers, which means that all solutions would require self-policing. And if you expect corrupt people to end corruption, you're living in a fucking fantasyland.

The only answer is to elect qualified people who love their country but don't desire power and position. I'll provide ideas for solutions and strategies for changing our political environment in future chapters. Some of my thoughts may surprise you or seem rather extreme. But I truly believe that the only way we will see corruption subside in our country is to take fairly drastic measures to change the entire game of politics.

This polarization of political parties, this climate of blind allegiance and hatred, this world of cheap stereotypes and labels, and this game of power plays and fame chasing has turned our politics into a mockery. It's a disgrace to the brilliant minds that built our government. And it has greatly weakened our nation. Is it any wonder that we want to escape our reality? Is it a surprise that we're sick, angry, and depressed?

In a nation that exalts victimhood and hardship, offers a hundred ways to choose ease over achievement, and is led by leaders hungry for power at all costs, are we surprised that we are where we are?

Anyone with access to the internet, or open ears for that matter, can recognize the fire of corruption and hypocrisy ablaze in our society. Unfortunately, there is also dangerously powerful gasoline being administered to this fire on a daily basis.

And that is what I want to talk about next.

CHAPTER 3

★

ESCAPING THE ECHO CHAMBER

September 11, 2001, was a warm day, as most are in San Diego. I tossed a couple of things inside my 1996 VW Jetta and headed down Interstate 5. At twenty-three, I was a part of SEAL Team 3 and had returned from deployment earlier that year. We were forming up another platoon, and I was feeling anxious to deploy again.

I tapped on the steering wheel and then cranked up the radio as I cruised down the highway, my mind wandering as I listened. Until I heard words that sent a shock wave. In horror, I sat there as reports of an attack on the World Trade Centers in New York came pouring in. It was hard to wrap my head around what I was hearing. I felt fear, rage, and uncertainty. Of all the scenarios my mind could have conjured up, of all the dangers I could have imagined our country facing, planes crashing into skyscrapers hadn't crossed my mind.

I know that the same shock wave I felt raced through the hearts and minds of every other American as we watched the news in collective horror, not only on that day but in the weeks and months that followed. *If a plane could be hijacked and driven into a skyscraper, what could happen next?* Our minds couldn't have foreseen an attack so terrifyingly creative, and suddenly we felt as though anything was possible—in the worst of ways. In the months that came after the attack, we glued ourselves to the television, radio, and internet, watching the news constantly...

...and that is when the twenty-four-hour news cycle was truly born.

Gone were the days of Walter Cronkite and a quick evening news special to finish out the day. Americans watched and listened nonstop. That single event redefined how most Americans spent a large portion of their free time. And while I don't think that anyone in our nation felt glee over the 9/11 tragedy, it is a fair and objective statement to say that the media flourished as a result of it. The fear and uncertainty that 9/11 elicited created a voracious appetite for news like never before. In terms of ratings and advertisement and the money that follows both, they hit the jackpot.

Overnight, it became an all-hands-on-deck situation as the media worked quickly to respond to the demand. Programs were created to fill every hour of the day. There had to be an early shift from 4:00–6:00 a.m., followed by a breakfast crew, then the morning news, followed by the afternoon crew, and then, of course, an all-star lineup for the evening and into the night.

All those initial feelings of rage, shock, horror, and fear that people experienced post-9/11 subsided as time moved on. But the media couldn't let their captive audience slip away that quickly. A demand had been created, and they couldn't let that die down. People just needed a reason to keep watching, listening, and reading. And so, in the years that followed, the media brilliantly provided just that: a reason to keep watching, listening, and reading.

Around the same time, the internet exploded with nuclear force. People suddenly carried their own personal television, radio set, and access to every newspaper and article they could ever want to read in their pocket. People could connect to news and information instantly with just the flick of a thumb. They only needed a reason to want to pull it out (there's gotta be a good *that's what she said* somewhere in that sentence).

So let me ask you this: what is the most effective way to get people to watch the news, listen to the radio, or scroll the latest headlines on their phones? Because that's the exact question that the media was asking themselves in the wake of such a massive surge in popularity along with a collective, "Holy shit! How do we keep this going?"

So let's break it down. When you're sitting on your couch at home and you see something on the news that angers you, what do you do? You yell at the TV. You get pissed off.

But you keep watching.

When you see a headline that scares the shit out of you, what do you do? Well, for starters, you're sure as fuck not grabbing the remote and turning off the television. Nobody looks at the television, reads a headline, and thinks, "Oh, the world's going to end? Hmmmm, I think now's a good time to switch channels and watch a soap opera."

Hell no. You're going to stop what you're doing, and you're going to stay glued to that screen. You're going to turn on the radio in the kitchen while you make breakfast. You're going to pull up *The Washington Post* on your phone and skim it while you take a shit. And you know what?

Pissed off and scared people are the most captive audience.

Think about the kind of stuff news anchors say right before a commercial break. "Next up: Is your next-door neighbor a rapist? And should we be concerned about the new virus that has popped up in Africa? We'll cover that plus the startling connection between toothpaste and cancer with an expert in the field when we come back."

Cheesy smiles flash white teeth, the music crescendos, and you and every other motherfucker out there listening suddenly need to know if your neighbor is a rapist, if there's another epidemic on the horizon, and if your toothpaste is giving you cancer.

And it's not just televised news. Headlines, news feeds, and radio sound bites all center around inflammatory one-liners and titles that make you feel angry or scared. With so many sources to go to for news online, the competition is fiercer than ever. Just reporting the facts and events of the day isn't going to cut it anymore—especially for televised news outlets. That means that to get an audience, you've got to have bigger, scarier headlines or more entertaining, captivating anchors that draw people into your content.

But the problem with humans is that the interesting things yesterday aren't going to hold your attention tomorrow.

You see this exemplified in many areas. Whether it's drugs, sex/pornography, adrenaline chasing, or high-speed racing, the first time you dip your toe in the water, you feel a sense of wonder and thrill. Anything that is just a notch above normal life feels exciting. Your heart pounds, your palms get sweaty, and you experience a rush. But then it dies down. And it's going to take just a little bit more to seduce that response out of you again.

The adrenaline junkie starts as a guy just jumping off a front porch deck into a pool. Now that's no Evel Knievel bullshit, but it sure as fuck is going to get the heart rate pumping the first time if that deck is high enough. Fast-forward five years, and that same guy is BASE jumping illegally off a building in downtown Manhattan. How did he make that jump (no pun intended) from decks to buildings? It resulted from needing just a little bit more adrenaline, a little bit more danger each time to give him the same high, leading him to constantly up the ante.

Someone pops a couple tramadol pills for a backache and ends up mainlining heroin five years later because feeling "good" isn't good enough after a while. The stimulus of the pills wears off, and something stronger is needed to achieve the same feeling and get the same response.

Remember the first time you stumbled on your dad's collection of nudie magazines? Or saw people fucking for the first time on a porno? Your eyes got huge, and you had that moment of awestruck wonder thinking, "Oh shit! So that's what it looks like." One look, and you're ready to go on the spot. Fast-forward a decade, and unless it's some full-blown, aggressively explicit, whips and chains, gang-bang porno, it's just not going to do it for you, and suddenly Dad's nudie mags look more like classy artwork. What was once shocking and stimulating becomes forgettable and boring.

I've found the same true for fast cars—something that I've dabbled in a bit myself in the past few years. As a kid, I didn't give a shit about fast cars. I wasn't the kid with posters of Lamborghinis on my walls. But over the past several years, I've gotten hooked as I've delivered dogs to people all over the nation who have large collections of fast cars and the inclination to toss me the keys and say, "Take her for a spin." The first time I drove a car that was marginally faster than a run-of-the-mill commuter car, I thought, "Holy Fuck! This is incredible." But next thing I know, flooring a $500,000 Lamborghini isn't enough to get my blood pumping because I've grown too accustomed to high speeds, and I find myself thinking about how to supercharge it so I can feel that shockwave again.

These are just a few examples of human nature on display: we always want more. Whether it's horror movies with gallons of splattered blood or the creation of a triple-decker, bacon-filled, cheese-slathered, three-meat-patty burger with a donut bun, we will find a way to constantly up the ante. Because every time the thrill of something new dies down, the bar for normal goes a little bit higher—causing the criteria for something to be considered extraordinary to be even higher than that.

And this is exactly what has happened in the media.

After the demand was created for twenty-four-hour news in the wake of 9/11, the media has worked to hold onto that audience. But what scared people into clicking on the link or watching another hour of news isn't doing it anymore. What angered people into social media comment battles last month doesn't even cause a blip of emotion today. People always want more.

And this is where the real trouble started.

The goal of news outlets is no longer just about presenting you with news reports to keep you thoughtfully informed. Anyone with access to the internet can obtain information and reports on breaking news. And media outlets know that. This means that their primary job is not simply providing you with information but packaging it in a way that makes you want to get your news from them rather than someone else. It became about getting you to watch *their* show or read *their* publication or listen to *their* radio station.

And this is how the chaotic shitstorm of biased media, all clamoring for a moment in the spotlight, began. It started with the twenty-four-hour news cycle and the explosion of the internet and morphed into a vicious contest to see who can best capture and hold people's attention. The truth is that if the media just presented you with a completely objective, unbiased daily report, the news would get pretty boring pretty fast, and there would be absolutely no need for the multitude of news sources. But if one outlet gives you your news out of the mouth of a prettier person, you might just choose to watch that station over another. Or if this talk show host makes you laugh a little harder at the expense of the political party you disagree with, you might just choose them over another.

With the rise of the internet, the competition for capturing the American public's attention became a ferocious business. No matter how much a news outlet wants you to believe that the network that *you* choose to watch is the only blameless, trustworthy, and reliable example of fair journalism left in the world, the truth is, there's not one that is much better than the rest.

No one can successfully make it on a middle-of-the-road, just-here-to-give-you-the-facts kind of platform. Gone are the days of middle-aged men with mustaches and raspy voices giving you an hour of the evening news. To maintain popularity, you need to appeal to a *target audience*. You need to make it your job to keep that target audience watching, tuning in, and reading, which sounds harmless enough at first. But the entire basis of this kind of thinking means that a calculated assessment and decision have to be made as to *who will make up that target audience and who won't*. Once that is established, it's more or less your job to pander to your core group of followers, viewers, and listeners—even if it's at the expense of another audience. Calculated risks have to be taken because the thing that makes one audience clap may evoke boos from others. But filtering, packaging, and presenting the news with a target audience in mind is a dangerous business.

Now, not only is the media filled with a constant quest to provide news that is more angering or frightening than before—causing gross exaggerations and cherry-picked headlines—it has also become an echo chamber. Because people love hearing their own opinions, points of view, and beliefs mirrored back to them. And nothing ensures a loyal consumer more than doing just that.

That's why news outlets have become experts in carefully selecting topics that will interest, scare, or enrage their target audience. They know how to report things in a way that reinforces your beliefs so that you feel vindicated and justified, and hold your head up a little higher throughout your day, knowing that you are *on the right side.*

They know how to infuriate you with sound bites of your favorite political nemesis and spin stories to give you another reason to hate them. Because, believe it or not, you actually love to hate. Like it or not, it's exciting to hate someone, and most people will jump at any chance they get to do so. Don't believe me? I'd bet some solid money that there's an annoying friend from high school that you stalk on social media just because seeing their face pop up on your news feed all fat and divorced makes you feel a little happy.

Media outlets know that it's reassuring to hear your own political opinions repeated through the mouths of brilliant, funny, and accomplished people—making you feel surer of yourself. They know how validating it is for you to immerse yourself in a choir of like-minded people and preach your truth and convince yourself of it a little bit more with every word. They provide you with just such a context.

Despite what anyone says, most people don't *actually* want to have their viewpoints challenged, their perspectives changed, or their beliefs called into question. They don't actually want to be presented with compelling truths on two sides of an issue and have to think for themselves. They just want to feel like they are in the know and on the right side. The winning side. The side that makes sense.

And as much as you may want to believe that your favorite news station reports *the real facts* and *the real truth*, there's a very high possibility that you think that simply because they report a version of the truth that most resonates with you. Have you ever thought about the fact that *you* might just be the target audience that they are catering to? Few people recognize their own bias and therefore *tend to mistake the unbiased truth for the one that simply matches their viewpoint.*

These echo chambers filled with hatred, anger, fear, chaos, and mass hysteria keep people glued to their news outlet of choice. And with a whole industry dedicated and motivated to perpetuate these things, it's no wonder people can't see and reason clearly or even calm down long enough to have an honest conversation—let alone form any kind of objective opinion or innovative solution to our problems. Is it any surprise that our politics have become so polarized and chaotic?

Additionally, with the rise of celebrity media figures who have millions of followers and more influence than ever before, the ability to sway people with a single individual's personal opinions and beliefs is rising dangerously. You have people of power like Mark Zuckerberg, Jeff Bezos, and Jack Dorsey, who have enough money never to have to work another day in their life, but they are still running strong. Why? I believe it's because they are addicted to the power and influence they have. They are in a position to make decisions that will shape our future and our children's future. They have the power to shape the way our freedoms are translated into the digital age as censorships are put into place and information is monitored. We will take a deeper look at our nation's idolatry of celebrities more in a later chapter. Still, it's worth noting that the way we have erected celebrity gods and goddesses out of news anchors and journalists, business owners, and politicians has some serious downsides and is only creating more bias and opportunity for greed and lust for power to permeate our society.

What has all of this led to?

It's led to exactly where we are today. A time where *everyone is inundated with information yet objectively uninformed*. A time where everyone is screaming out their opinions simply to hear them reverberated in their echo chambers with others doing the same. A time where journalism has become an embarrassing pissing competition for who has more party tricks and scary headlines to win the audience.

It's also led to something that is possibly even more concerning—the desensitization of our society. In a world inundated with media that is constantly upping the ante to grab the public's attention, people have become numb and desensitized.

When everything is an outrage, nothing is.

Far too many people have become so accustomed to overconsuming media—to the shocking headlines and warnings of doom and destruction just on the horizon that they cease to feel much of anything anymore. People are so accustomed to feeling constant anger, hatred, and fear that it's become a normal part of life. Between music, movies, television, and the ocean of information on the internet, even atrocities have become normalized due to our constant exposure to them. A favorite quote of mine perfectly sums up the danger that this places our society in:

"Whoever fights monsters should see to it that in the process he does not become a monster. And if you gaze long enough into an abyss, the abyss will gaze back into you."

—Friedrich Nietzsche

Sadly, people are unaware of the factors in play that constantly manipulate their perceptions, that create shouting matches out of what could have been a civil conversation, that polarize politics and normalize atrocity and chaos. This leaves our society more vulnerable than ever. People have never been so addicted to staring into the abyss, and I am afraid of what will happen when the abyss gazes back.

I began this book by saying that we needed to have some conversations about issues that matter in our world, like our border, human trafficking, our economy, and much more. So why start by talking about the media? Because we will never be able to honestly discuss any important issue until we realize that we've allowed ourselves to be swayed and influenced by a media that capitalizes on and reinforces our fear, anger, and biases. We must come to the table with open minds. And having an open, independent mind these days is not something that happens easily.

No one is immune to the brainwashing effects of our media. I'm not, and you're not. Liberals aren't, and conservatives aren't. It takes vigilance, effort, and bravery to maintain the independence of thought, belief, and opinion these days. And it will not happen until we extract ourselves from the echo chambers that we've been living in. Until we remove the biased perceptions that the media has perpetuated and we have willingly surrendered to. Until we refuse to be one more screeching gong in the symphony of chaos.

Unfortunately, changing this media environment, just like our political climate, will not happen easily. Change will not happen by adding more regulations or by news outlets calling out their opposition. Change will only happen when media outlets are actually willing to police their own and hold themselves accountable and to the same standards that they place on their competition. Change will only occur when enough individuals think for themselves, take action, and stop playing the goddamn game. As with most problems in our nation, the answer to this problem lies in the hands of the fucking people.

You and I may not be able to reform an entire system or quiet down the mob of screaming people, but we sure as hell can control our own minds. How does that look practically? I have several suggestions on practices you can put into place that are simple but effective in maintaining independent thought and doing your part to help change this aspect of our society. They are things that I have put into practice in my own life and still strive to keep at the forefront of my mind daily. These are also vital prerequisites that we need to have in place before discussing the important issues that are ahead.

1. Take it upon yourself to discern what is bullshit and what is not. Be open to the fact that you may already be

knee-deep in bullshit and don't even know it. Be honest
and don't practice such blind allegiance to a political
party or news outlet that you can't smell the stench of
what you stepped in.

2. Spend as much time researching, corroborating, and
   verifying the information you receive as you do taking
   it in. Don't just believe something because you want to
   believe it or because you like the person who is telling you
   to believe it. If you *want* to believe it or if you *really like* the
   person telling you to believe it, you should be researching
   it even harder—knowing your own propensity toward bias.

3. Listen, watch, and read news from varied sources
   and outlets. It's important to have as much of a well-
   rounded perspective as possible. It won't be perfect
   or unbiased, but it will be far better than being glued
   to one fucking channel or media outlet and spoon-fed
   information without taking a deeper look at what's
   being presented to you.

4. Vote with your wallet. If you fundamentally disagree with
   the basis of a platform, stop using it. Don't engage it and
   don't take part in creating a demand for it. Hold media
   outlets accountable and call them out for dishonesty.

5. Don't take it upon yourself to regurgitate everything
   you hear. Don't hit the share or forward button within

thirty seconds of skimming an article or watching a video. Doing so only furthers a biased agenda and creates more of a divide. Some things need to be said, and some information needs to be shared. But a whole shitload of it doesn't. Be discerning.

I hope by this point in our conversation the fog is starting to lift a little bit. I hope you're starting to feel a power shift take place. I hope you're putting the power back in your own fucking hands and putting a stop to the ways you've allowed outside sources to manipulate and shape your opinions, emotions, and beliefs. I also hope that this chapter has shed some light on one of the largest contributing factors to our nation finding itself in the position it is in today. There are a few other aspects of the media that we will cover more in later chapters—such as the worship of celebrities and our culture of hypocrisy and virtue signaling. But before that, we've got to talk about another element that has made a generous contribution to the weakened society we have today.

And you may not like it.

Not going to lie, this may be a touchy subject, and you know I'm not about to give the truth a sugar rubdown or drizzle it with fucking Hershey's syrup. Somebody's got to be the first to address the elephant in the room. Somebody's got to be the first one to raise their hand and ask the question we're all thinking.

"Who the hell raised this generation?"

And it looks like that somebody is going to be me.

*

CHAPTER 4

WHO THE HELL RAISED THESE KIDS?

s we look to identify the factors that brought us to where we are as a society, it's easy to point the finger at the media or significant political and legislative decisions that have altered our culture. But there's another factor that, in my opinion, has had an even greater impact on society and its trajectory.

And that is parenting.

This chapter isn't about me being a grumpy old White guy with a bone to pick with millennials or Generation X, Y, Z, or whatever the fuck alphabetical letter you are. It is about carefully and honestly assessing the major factors that have created the state of our society today. If you bake a cake and it flops and tastes like shit, you might want to go back and look at the recipe and see what ingredients you put in there so you don't do it again.

As we gape at unsettling statistics on mental and physical health and the level of education that the average American graduates high school with today, we can't just point the finger at the media or the government. We gotta turn that little motherfucker right back at ourselves and ask the tough questions: "Who the hell raised these kids that are now adults? Who raised the people that have created such alarming statistics on mental and physical health, the decline in education, and addiction of every kind?"

And I think we all know the answer.

The media, technology, and even our school systems aren't the only ones to blame for the weakening of our nation. According to the United States Census Bureau in 2016, most of America's 73.7 million children under age eighteen live in families with two parents (69 percent). The second most common family arrangement is children living with a single mother (23 percent). That means that overwhelmingly, American children are growing up under the guidance of *at least one of their parents.*

Parents are tasked with preparing and raising the next generation, and it's time that we hold ourselves accountable for that task. This accountability should manifest itself in us leading by example. To me, the ultimate test of character is when you do the right thing when nobody's watching except the tiny little faces that look up at you and call you Mom or Dad.

So if we see a lot of little dipshits running around, it's time we take a look in the mirror and realize that the dipshit might just be the one looking back at us.

As a parent, you are given a choice as to how you want to raise your child. It's entirely up to you. Whether you take an active role or a passive one, you are still molding and influencing the adults they will become. *You* are providing the environment in which they will be raised. Children are like sponges that soak in their surroundings, and it's up to you to determine what that is.

And if you're not leading by example, you're fucking doing it wrong.

Having said that, I want to make two things clear. First of all, there isn't and shouldn't be an idealistic standard when it comes to parenting. I believe that parents should have a significant amount of autonomy to raise their children how they see fit. Everyone will have a different way to lead by example and a different version of what that example is. And that's okay. At the bare minimum, I think we can all agree that we should be raising them to be an asset and not a liability to society. It doesn't matter *what* they are contributing to society; it just matters that they contribute *something* positive. Not all kids are meant to be fucking brain surgeons, high-level politicians who shape our nation and influence policy, or Michelin Star chefs. But at the very least, every parent should mold and shape their child to be a contributing member of our society.

Secondly, I want to be the first to say that I have made a shitload of mistakes as the father of two daughters and am by no means holding myself up as a standard of perfection. In fact, much of the perspective that I will offer here results from looking back over the last fifteen plus years and seeing mistakes that I made as a parent. I've had to force myself to take inventory of my own parenting choices over the years, identify my failings, and be brave enough to admit them. I've made choices that I regret as a parent, choices I'm ashamed of, and there are many things I wish I could take back or change.

But as much as I'll be the first to confess that I've done a lot of things wrong, I've also done some things right. Over time I have seen that even the mistakes I made played a part in forming the two strong, independent young women I get to call my daughters and made me a better father as I have learned from them. However, I'm by no means a perfect parent, and I know firsthand how goddamn hard it is to raise kids. So don't think for a second that I'm sitting on a high horse or giving you thoughts and opinions that haven't been tested in the real world.

My awareness of my own imperfections doesn't negate the fact that I have very strong opinions about raising children. I do lay much of the responsibility for the state of our society at the feet of parents—a responsibility that I place on myself right along with every other parent in the last several decades. As demonstrated through the alarming statistics that we discussed in the first chapter, this weakened society shows a downward spiral that is inextricably correlated to the way we parent and raise our children.

The top four holes that I see in modern parenting are below.

PROBLEM 1: A LACK OF LEADING BY EXAMPLE

There is a troubling lack of parents leading by example today. And this is a big problem. If you attempt to get a child to do something that you don't do yourself, it presents many challenges. Children emulate what they see. So, if you aren't practicing what you preach, you're already working uphill by demonstrating behaviors/habits that you do or don't want them to practice. And if you give them the old "do as I say, not as I do," this only creates resentment toward you—a resentment which often causes children to act out in spite.

They will push back, break the rules, and sneak around out of anger toward your double standards. Nobody wants to work hard for a hypocrite, and children can spot bullshit a mile away. Far too many parents are unwilling to hold themselves to the same standards that they want to hold their children to. How many parents expect their child to be healthy, active, smart, patient, hardworking, and kind while they stuff their faces with fast food, don't get outside or exercise, don't read or continue to learn and expand their knowledge, have a short fuse and a bad temper, lie on the couch after work for hours on their phone, and speak rudely to those around them? Children *must* be led by example, and there is a staggering lack of it in our society.

PROBLEM 2: A LACK OF PROVIDING THE RESOURCES TO SET CHILDREN UP FOR SUCCESS

Any parent will bitch and moan about how expensive having kids is, but few put time and thought into truly investing in their child the same way they would a 401(k), mutual fund, or real estate. Every investment made in the next generation is an investment in our nation's future. And yet, far too many parents spend their time, money, and resources on things that deprive a child of an environment in which he or she can thrive. As a result, the parent shortchanges both the child and themselves. That doesn't mean that parents can't have nice things or treat themselves to life's pleasures, but those things should never take priority over giving a child everything they need to succeed. If a child is missing out on getting to do an art project, join a band, or pursue a sport or hobby due to financial limits while the parent slaps new rims on their vehicle or purchases a new gun, that parent is an asshole and is fucking wrong. And there are far too many selfish asshole parents out there raising selfish asshole kids.

PROBLEM 3: A LACK OF PROPER BOUNDARIES AND OPPORTUNITY FOR CHILDREN TO FAIL AND LEARN

The last major lack I see in parents today is setting and enforcing proper discipline and boundaries and the opportunity for the child to fail and learn from their mistakes. One of the primary ways children learn is by trying and failing—by making their own mistakes, feeling the pain of their consequences, and correcting their behavior to ensure it doesn't happen again.

Now, that doesn't mean that parents should let their two-year-old wander onto the freeway to learn that cars are dangerous. Still, it does mean that children *must be allowed the freedom to try and fail*, to bump up against strongly enforced rules and boundaries, and face the consequences of bad behavior. Most parents are too afraid to enforce discipline or take a step back and let their child make a mistake or fail at something and learn from it.

The term "helicopter parent" was coined in the last couple of decades and very aptly describes many parents today. They hover over their child, fearful that they will do the wrong thing. They shield them from failure, disappointment, or bearing the consequences of their own poor choices. This parenting style has yielded some pretty shitty results, and it's evident as we watch these children reach adulthood. We are releasing eighteen-year-old fucking infants into society who have been raised in a bubble that cushions them from the harsh realities of the real world. And our society is suffering because of it.

But it wasn't always this way.

The American parenting methodology has shifted in the past several decades—significantly in the '90s and early 2000s. This change in our parenting paradigm is perhaps one of the greatest shifts that has ever taken place culturally in our society. While medical and technological advancement has certainly impacted our culture, it holds no comparison to the impact that our shifting parental paradigm and methodology have had. I'd like to pull at this thread a little bit and see if we can identify when and how this shift began.

If you were to talk to one of your parents, grandparents, or the oldest little man or woman you can find and ask them what life was like when they were a child, what would they say? Within minutes, you'd see a drastic difference between the way their lives looked and the average child's does today. You'd see it manifested in everything from what they were allowed to do, the level of independence given to them, the expectations placed upon them, and even what they ate and did with their free time. One of the greatest differences you'd see is that *parents were given far more autonomy to raise their children as they saw fit and thus took on the responsibility to do so.*

As we've talked about, the road to hell is paved with good intentions. In the last several decades, there has been a lot of awareness for and action taken against child abuse. We can all agree that fighting violence against innocent children is a worthy endeavor. The intent is pure and good-hearted and many of the measures that have been put into place to ensure that children are not neglected or mistreated are also good. But as with any shift in society, the propensity toward overcorrection is always there.

Now, outside agencies and their service members hold the power to remove children from their homes if they feel that it is necessary. Oftentimes, these decisions are necessary. But as time goes on, as with anything, there is a slippery slope that leads to a result that is a far cry from what was intended. We've gone from simply having measures in place to remove children from abusive homes to a system where children can complain to a teacher about a parent hurting their feelings and next thing you know, the parents are being interviewed by Child Protective Services and are in danger of losing their children.

You hear stories of kids suing their parents or filing for emancipation and it being granted under circumstances when neither one should be allowed. As is true with issues such as drugs, guns, prostitution, etc., when the government steps in and decides to regulate the shit out of human behavior, it creates problems when taken too far. No one would argue a case for banishing the laws and regulations to protect the innocent. Still, we must also be mindful and careful that we don't allow our lives to become micromanaged by the government.

This micromanaging creates resentment and pushback in some people, fear and tentativeness in others. Some push against the constraints and regulations or become masters at keeping their evil deeds under a blanket of secrecy while others—I'd say the majority—walk on eggshells, deathly afraid to do anything at all. It's the worst of both extremes. Parents are so afraid that they will get in trouble because their kid fucked up and they'll be viewed as a neglectful or horrible parent that they micromanage every decision their child makes. *And this fear is what birthed the helicopter parent.*

The fear of making a mistake or doing it wrong, the fear of being viewed as a bad parent and knowing the dire consequences that could come as a result, has left most parents timid and immobilized. As outside agencies are given more and more power to regulate parents, it has caused many parents to relinquish their sense of responsibility to raise their children—assuming that others will do it for them.

In addition to parents being scared to parent, most are incredibly underprepared and uneducated on being a good parent. As we talked about before, any area in life that you desire success in takes preparation, research, and time to develop a capacity to excel. Raising children well is not a task that anyone should take lightly. Parents need to be educated on and equipped with how to do it well. Which speaks to my next point.

PROBLEM 4: A LACK OF KNOWLEDGE AND UNDERSTANDING OF HOW TO PROPERLY RAISE A CHILD

Parenting, as with anything you want to become good at or proficient in, requires education, knowledge, and expanded understanding. When you find out that you are expecting a child, you have a good bit of time to prepare for it. We're not like rabbits who have twenty-seven days to get ready to birth a whole litter. On average, you usually have a good nine months to prepare for the responsibility of raising one child.

Nowadays, unfortunately, there's more thought, money, and time put into picking out a paint color for the nursery or doing some grandiose fucking gender reveal party than there is actually preparing to raise the kid. Producing an educated, socially comfortable, productive member of society does not happen by accident. Any good parent can attest to the amount of time, resources, and knowledge it takes to do just that. And it's something that parents need to take more seriously. If you want to get your body in shape, have a well-trained dog, become proficient in playing an instrument, or earn a black belt in jujitsu, you've got to devote yourself to learning and equipping yourself with everything you need to excel. Far too many parents are either naive, lazy, or arrogant to self-educate and prepare for what is required to raise a child well and it shows.

Instead of the government mandating and micromanaging, there should be more efforts to educate parents successfully and set them up to raise positive, contributing members of society. Parents need to be educated on a child's need for proper nutrition, exercise, and mental stimulation. Parents need helpful strategies on how to interact with their children meaningfully and handle difficult situations that arise when answers are not black and white.

In this day and time, there's more preparation and oversight to get a driver's license, install a swimming pool, or adopt a dog than to become a parent. That's absurd. I'm not saying it should be harder to have kids. It's a free country and it's your choice to procreate. It's just absurd that for all the stupid shit this country spends money on and creates programs and initiatives for, we don't have more resources available to educate and prepare parents for raising competent adults. There is far more money spent on things that are far less important. And that is a travesty. After all, they are the future of this nation. They are the ones that we will pass the torch to when our time is done.

I would like to emphasize very clearly that more assistance does *not* mean that we need more regulations. Quite the contrary. This assistance must be created and handled correctly—without allowing vultures to swoop in and use it as an opportunity to further an agenda of any kind. These resources cannot be FDA, USDA, and Big Pharma influenced—promoting shitty food and medications that will just fuck your kids up while they make a buck. That's not going to help anybody.

We need a solid program that equips, prepares, and educates parents on raising children. I'm talking about legitimate, science-backed, research-based materials and resources created by experts and psychologists not funded or incentivized by lobbyists from large food and drug companies. Resources created by unbiased third parties with a proven track record.

There are countless ways that such assistance could be provided to parents and this is an area that could benefit greatly from the use of technology. Providing free online classes, forums, and resources for parents would be a perfect way to make quality resources readily available. I have seen firsthand how much dog owners have gravitated toward my online dog training model and benefited from having guidance and education from a qualified source provided conveniently. The same basic idea could be implemented for providing parents with quality education and resources.

Some might argue that people don't need guidance to know how to be a parent. I'd like to think that's true, but a quick look around at many parents today and the result of their methods would tell me otherwise. Some people need to be told that putting Coca-Cola into a fucking bottle and giving it to a nine-month-old is probably not a good idea. Some need to be coached on how to provide constructive boundaries. Some need resources to learn about the necessary elements of health, safety, and education that create an environment for a child to thrive. And just about everyone could use a little direction on parenting through the teenage years and navigating the process of launching a child into thriving adulthood.

Again, this assistance should be coupled with autonomy. Parents should have access to basic tools on raising healthy, functioning members of society and then be given the freedom to implement that in their own way. It goes without saying that this autonomy excludes provision for child abuse or neglect. It should provide parents information and tools and then allow them to take ownership of child-rearing and do it their way without fear.

If we hope to change the course of our nation, if we hope to reverse the statistics we read about today, if we hope to create a more peaceful, strong, educated, successful society, we have to change the way we are raising future generations. I want to share a few ways to immediately begin that process if you have children of your own. This is coming from a very imperfect father who's made a shitload of mistakes like anyone else. Some of this advice has been born out of regrets and lessons learned through failure. Some of it has been born out of things that I have seen proven to be very successful. All of it has been tested out in real situations and real life. I believe these are the things that will make the greatest positive impact on the next generation if implemented.

SELF-EVALUATE

First, take a good, hard look at where you and your kids are at *right now*. Where are you succeeding? Where are you failing? Don't sugarcoat it or make excuses. Be honest. Don't be what we refer to in the dog industry as "kennel blind." If your kids were somebody else's, would you look at them and think, "God, what a bunch of little dipshits; I'd love to punch their parents in the face"?

If the answer is yes, you've got some work to do. Take inventory of how your child is doing in all aspects of life and then do the same for yourself. Don't place yourself under an expectation of perfection but be willing to own up to where your child is lacking and your part in contributing to that. Can you look at yourself in the mirror at the end of the day and know that you are doing the very best you can with what you have as a parent? Can you honestly say that you are leading by example?

If you see shortcomings and failures, acknowledge where you are coming up short and then form a strategy to improve. Assess the things you are doing well and continue to excel in those areas but put forth effort to grow and improve where you're falling short. Educate yourself, get the resources you need, and seek advice from experienced and proven sources if you need to. Do whatever it takes to improve where needed.

GIVE KIDS INDEPENDENCE AND LET THEM FALL ON THEIR ASS SOMETIMES

Parents today are far too scared of giving their kids independence for fear that they will fail, experience disappointment, or get hurt. This means that children are often woefully underprepared for the harsh realities of the real world. There is a lot of talk about anti-bullying campaigns, sensitivities, political correctness, and equal outcomes for every child. So much so, it seems we've made it our mission in life to shield our children from the real world. We are churning out far too many eighteen-year-old infants who have never had to deal with real life because we've placed them in a protective bubble. To those kids I want to say, "Sure it sucks when a kid is mean to you at school, but guess what, fuckface? That's real life. It's going to kick you in the nuts, it's going to be unfair, it's going to knock you down and hurt your feelings. That's just the world we live in."

Far too many of the poor coping mechanisms that we see in adults today are simply the result of being unprepared for the world. Kids benefit from having to face disappointment, failure, and ridicule while still under the guidance of a parent to help them navigate it and learn from it.

If you have a kid who thinks that the best way to deal with negative circumstances is to complain until someone else fixes it, they've got one hell of a shitstorm coming their way. Because bitching about life and waiting for someone to step in and fix everything will only make things worse. It's an incredible disservice to raise a child in a protected little pocket, with every minute of his day planned out, every decision micromanaged, and then throw him out into the world and expect him to thrive.

There have been many times that one of my daughters has come to me with a situation or problem they are facing, and I'll ask them how they plan to handle it. They will tell me, and I'll listen quietly—knowing good and well that their approach will likely fail. I'll offer up my advice and how I would handle the situation if I were in their shoes. Then I'll ask if my thoughts change their position. They will often tell me that it didn't change their mind and they still feel that their approach is best. I don't push or belabor my points or opinions, I simply say, "Okay, if that's how you'd like to handle this and you feel confident in your choice, you have my full support." When they come back to me and tell me that their plan failed and want to know how to fix it, I don't jump in and take over. I sit back, let it be a teachable moment, and say, "You got into this situation, and now it's up to you to get out of it."

They don't always make the best choices and as a parent it's hard to watch them experience pain, disappointment, and failure. But it's a disservice not to allow them to. Sometimes this means letting your child fail a class, get in trouble at school, get kicked off of a sports team, lose a friendship, or get detention.

From the perspective of an entrepreneur, I can tell you that the two things that set apart successful people from the droves who attempt to be and fail are: possessing the ability to face problems and being resourceful enough to fix them, and knowing how to deal with failure and persevere when things get tough. We cannot rob our children of those two benchmark qualities. Fostering a safe environment in which they can both try and succeed as well as try and fail is crucial to raising successful adults. Failure is a brilliant teacher, one we cannot afford to silence.

CREATE AN ENVIRONMENT FOR LEARNING LIFE LESSONS AT HOME

There are many practical and easy ways to foster a home environment that will prepare children for the real world. I'll give you an example from my own parenting. There is a system for chores that I've used with my kids that has proven to be incredibly effective in teaching and reinforcing a whole list of valuable life skills and lessons. It's taught responsibility, independence, the correlation between actions and consequence, and the value of the dollar. Here's how it works:

First, I created a list of chores that I call the "Prerequisite List." This checklist includes cleaning their room, bathroom, and the common areas that they frequently use, putting their laundry away, etc. These items are a requirement for living under my roof and my children do not get paid for completing these tasks. It is simply the minimum responsibility for being a functional member of the household.

In addition, I made a list of chores that I call the "Extracurricular List." This includes things like yard work, scooping up the dog shit in the backyard, cleaning out the garage, etc. Each of these chore items has an amount of money attached to it—money I will pay for completing the task if it is done up to my standards. These are things my kids can do to earn extra money. The only caveat is that *all* items on their Prerequisite List must be completed *before* doing jobs on the Extracurricular List. If they clean the garage while their room is a mess, they will not get paid for the garage cleaning.

As my kids have reached the teenage years and want to have a cell phone, money to go out with friends, shopping funds, or extra cash to blow on snacks, they are expected to earn the money required for those purchases. If they want a cell phone, they have to earn that forty dollars a month to pay for it. If they want to get ice cream with their friends, they have to earn it. And I've laid out a very straightforward and easy way for them to do so. They just have to manage their time well, be responsible, and work hard. Do I need the extra forty dollars? Not really. But the lesson here is invaluable for them as they grow. Of course, there are circumstances in which I provide them with money to spend or float them a little cash, or just dote on them because I'm their dad and I love them. But for the majority of the time, we stick to this model.

This whole system has several benefits. First and foremost, they learn that it's *their actions that dictate outcome*. The correlation between their choices and the outcome of a situation is a simple yet powerful lesson to learn. If I have to take away one of my daughters' phones for a month because she didn't do the work required to pay for it, she doesn't have to ask why. She knows it's because of her own choices and you bet your ass she is going to ensure that she sees to her responsibilities the next time around. Secondly, this system eliminates the need for nagging, reminding, or getting into a power struggle with your child in an attempt to get them to do their chores. Lastly, it teaches them the value of the dollar and reinforces that money and reward are the result of hard work which, in turn, creates a strong sense of appreciation for the things they have.

There are many mechanisms and methods that could be used to teach similar lessons. Our duty as parents is to foster an environment to teach and prepare children for the world while they are still under our parental oversight. One of the greatest lessons they can learn is to think before they act and understand that actions have consequences. Again, this is simple but powerful. And sadly, this is very lacking in most of America's younger generation today.

DON'T RAISE A VICTIM

One of the things we discussed in a previous chapter was how our country has exalted the victim and created a culture saturated with the victimhood mentality. This comes with a sense of entitlement and the propensity to blame others for problems and look to someone else to find solutions to the challenges you face.

One of the greatest ways that I have seen this perpetuated lies in how parents teach their kids *not* to stand up for themselves. I've said it before, and I'll say it again: the road to hell is paved with good intentions. When schools started taking a severe antibullying stance, countless rules and regulations on student behavior followed. Many parents instilled the idea in their children that it *wasn't* okay to defend themselves out of fear that their child would get into trouble or be expelled.

"Nicely ask them to stop and if they don't, *don't* fight back and instead try to talk to a teacher about the situation once it's over."

That's the advice most parents give.

So why are we surprised that we have a culture of victimhood when we teach children from kindergarten up that it's not okay to stand up and defend themselves? I am very clear with my kids that if they are the ones to make the first move or start the fight, they will have me to deal with and there will be hell to pay. But if someone else affronts or attacks them, they are free to, and should, defend themselves. They know that I will stand by them and back them up in doing so.

When we teach kids *not* to do this, we teach them to relinquish an instinctual response for self-defense, hand over their power to an outside source, and wait for someone to come and fight their battles for them. When we teach kids to quite literally sit on their hands, do nothing, and call for help, it should come as no surprise that we have generations of adults who constantly complain, blame, and spend their lives waiting for someone or something to come along and make everything okay.

I am fully aware that not all schools tolerate actions taken—even in defense. I use this as an opportunity to teach my kids to do what is right and stand up for themselves even when others don't understand. My children know that I have their back and stand up for their decision to defend themselves to every teacher and principal if needed. If kids constantly complain and look to an outside source to provide for them, make the world fair, protect them, and make things easier, they will only perpetuate this behavior as adults.

The world is not a fair or perfect place and yet our society is on a quest to create a standard of perfection. And people become quickly disillusioned when that perfection is not reached. We fire people from jobs for making an offensive tweet on social media, for wearing clothing from brands with differing political views, and for countless other things that really shouldn't get you fired from a job. The quest for perfection has bled into school policy as our culture actively seeks to create a bubble for our children to learn and exist within—a place where no one gets their feelings hurt, everybody wins, no one feels excluded, and everyone is guaranteed the same outcome and success. This is a grave disservice to our children. The world will never be perfect, and life isn't a bubble. It's only a matter of time before someone will hurt their feelings, situations will be unfair, and they get knocked down. And it's our job as parents to prepare our children in such a way that they land on their feet and keep going when it does.

SET THE BAR

Like it or not, our kids are constantly watching and imitating our choices and behaviors. It's up to us as parents to set the bar. If we want to raise a strong generation, we have to set a strong example. If you're a cheating, lying motherfucker, don't be surprised if your kids turn out the same way. Do the right thing, even when you don't feel like it. Show them what it means to turn motivation into discipline by the way that you live your life. You can talk and preach to your kids all day about right and wrong, but *nothing* can replace leading by example.

INVEST YOUR RESOURCES TO SET THEM UP FOR SUCCESS

We already covered this, but I think it's worth saying again. As parents, it's our job to invest the resources necessary to set our kids up for success. That is going to mean different things for different people. For the parents out there who are of higher means, that doesn't mean that children should be given whatever the fuck they want. Teach them to earn their success through strategies like the one I implemented for chores outlined above. Teaching lessons like this are a far greater gift than any sum of money ever could be.

No matter how much money is in your bank account, use what you have and do everything you can to give your children resources to grow and thrive and provide them with an environment where they can learn and explore. Give them the tools needed to learn about things like hard work, the value of the dollar, and the correlation between action and consequences. Give them a taste of what it looks like and feels like to work hard and be successful.

DO YOUR BEST AND BE CONSISTENT

There is no such thing as a perfect parent. As parents, we make mistakes constantly. Through my journey of parenting daughters and navigating a divorce, I have had to learn a lot. I am incredibly proud of the example I have set for my children most of the time. I am ashamed at the example I have set other times. But as much as I hate screwing up, I also believe it's okay for children to see imperfections in their parents. It's okay that they see you make mistakes. Own it when you do, apologize, and seek to make true improvement. The key is to do your best and to be consistent.

As a dog trainer, I see a lot of parallels between dog training and raising kids. There are two ways to control a dog's behavior: the first is through punishment. In this method, you make things so uncomfortable or painful that they begin to do the things you want them to do due to the physical and mental pressure you are placing on them. This is not a positive way to learn or live. It's a shitty existence. Unfortunately, both dogs and humans are raised in this type of environment all the time and will never be able to reach their full potential because of it.

The second method is to train through primarily positive reinforcement with a strong emphasis on helping the dog understand that *their actions* will determine consequences. No matter what happens, they need to know and understand that their actions dictate the outcome of a situation. Once they understand that, it's like a light bulb goes off. They begin to think before they act.

Children are no different. It's important to create an environment where they can have that "light bulb" moment, an environment where it's easy to do the right thing and they are rewarded for it. When they don't do the right thing, they need someone to take the time to teach them and explain how they can avoid the same mistake next time.

Be consistent in your teaching and training. Allow your kids to make choices and face the consequences for them. Allow them to fall on their ass a few times and be there when it happens. Help them dust off and stand back up. Set an example for them and be humble enough to recognize areas that you need to grow in. Above all, do your best. With whatever means and abilities you have, invest in your children to the very best of your abilities.

Parenting has played a major role in shaping the trajectory of our nation. It's important to identify the part it's played in leading our culture to where it is today. We've made some mistakes and taken some wrong turns as a society and we need to be brave enough to admit that. The good news is that we have the power to make a shift in the right direction. By investing in our children's lives, we are investing in the future of our nation and planet.

Is there anything more important than that?

CHAPTER 5

★

JAY-Z ISN'T JESUS

W e've identified several things that have played a significant role in shaping our culture and contributing to the state we find our nation in today. So far we've talked about the birth of the twenty-four-hour news cycle, biased media, victimhood mentality, polarizing politics, and parenting. We're peeling back the layers and hopefully things are becoming a bit clearer. The next thing I'd like to talk about is the American celebrity culture and its impact on influencing our society.

Maybe you laughed at the title. But like it or not, America is a nation that prizes, or rather *worships*, celebrities of all types. From actors to professional athletes to entertainers, our culture exalts and idolizes them all. And as technology, TV, internet, and social media have expanded, so has the extent of their influence on our society. I think many people would like to think that they aren't enamored or persuaded by celebrities. Still, the truth is that these individuals have a far greater impact on our culture and political climate than we'd like to think. That's what I'd like to dive into next.

The term celebrity is a broad one so I'll specifically focus on two major categories of celebrities and the impact of each.

ACTORS, MUSICIANS, ENTERTAINERS, AND PROFESSIONAL ATHLETES

In the first category we have actors, musicians, entertainers, and professional athletes. There are other subcategories that you could also include here, but these cover a fairly broad spectrum. Think about the tremendous influence the men and women who fall under these categories have on our society today. Take a quick look around and you'll see that they often determine what our nation cares about, buys, is interested in, and even how we fix our hair and dress our bodies. They influence our political opinions and votes. They influence the standard by which we measure ourselves. They are the water and we are the sponge— soaking up their opinions and perspectives on the world through television, tabloids, and social media. This relatively small sect of the population influences the very large majority.

What's so wrong with being influenced by these individuals? They're beautiful, wealthy, and successful, aren't they? Is there anything more American than a good Hollywood celebrity or late-night entertainer? Who doesn't love a little J-Lo, Jimmy Fallon, Jay Leno, LeBron James, and the Kardashians in their lives? (Okay, maybe a handful of us *could* do without the Kardashians.)

The biggest problem is that *the celebrities with the most influence on everyday people do not live everyday lives.* They live in a world where what they look like, who they hang out with, what products they use, what they wear, and what car they drive is of paramount importance. These kinds of superficial things are everything to them. And hey, if you've gotten to that point in your life and career where those are the biggest cares you have, more power to you. Live your life. I've got no problem with it. But for the rest of society, these things should be the *small* and *inconsequential* parts of our lives. However, due to the level of influence that celebrities have, their cares, concerns, and opinions have become ours. And it's skewed our sense of reality. We allow a small, elite group of individuals to alter what we care about and what we place in high regard.

People are influencing our society in areas where *they hold no real experience or expertise.* These individuals have achieved wealth and success based upon a very specific niche. They are proficient in and educated on an incredibly specialized talent. This is true of professional athletes who excel in a very narrow set of skills. If you want to learn how to throw, catch, run, or dunk, they're just the expert you're looking for. But if you're taking lessons from them on how to live your personal life or aligning your beliefs with them, you may want to look at their track record and realize that they aren't always the people you'd want to imitate off the field.

Actors also have a specific skill set. But take a second to think about what that *actually is.* They are superbly proficient *professional liars.* They are highly paid bullshit artists and pretenders.

And while any of us who love a good action movie or comedy on a Friday night appreciate their talents, we must keep in mind that their contribution to society is to entertain.

While that's a nice addition to our lives, it should not be mistaken for moral character or expertise. They are famous liars and entertainers, not productive members of society. Suppose some great apocalypse were to destroy our nation as we know it and we were forced to rebuild from scratch. Would Kim Kardashian have any valuable skill, knowledge, proficiency, or craft to contribute to the reconstruction of society? I think we all know the answer to that question.

These entertainers also do not possess expertise in politics. They are not equipped to solve our country's social issues. Their lifestyle and opinions should have little to no bearing on how the average person lives their life. And yet, our society holds these pretenders, these bullshit artists that don't really fucking *do* anything, in high regard—allowing their political affiliations, motivations, and agendas to supersede our own. We allow these elite entertainers to determine what is important to us, what we should spend our time doing, and what the standard of success is.

When rich, highly paid liars are among the greatest influencers of our lifestyle and politics, it's a scary situation. Is it any wonder that our country is so fucked up? Is it any wonder that our society has become that spoiled rich brat we talked about in Chapter 1?

Actors aren't inherently bad people, but they are a poor choice to place in any position of influence in our society. This is true for several reasons. First of all, they promote unrealistic standards. Because looks, aesthetics, and the way you present yourself are vastly important in the world of television and entertainment, actors and entertainers become experts or hire other experts to make them appear flawless when they show themselves to the world. When you see a shot in a movie, on the runway, or on the front cover of a magazine, you can bet your ass that the featured actor or actress didn't just roll out of bed looking that way. You don't know what starvation diet they went on to fit in that $500,000 runway gown. You don't know what crazy immersion workout camp he had to join to get his abs to look that way. You don't see the team of makeup artists prepping her for the photo, posing her, and airbrushing her skin. You don't see the extensive editing and Photoshopping that takes place before you look at that image on the front cover of a magazine while you're waiting in line at Target.

There are thousands upon thousands of dollars spent and hours invested just to make these famous bodies and faces appear a certain way. You only see them posed in perfect lighting and makeup and then feel inferior when you don't wake up looking like that on a regular Tuesday morning. Far too many people still hold this perception of perfection as the standard. This is both toxic and logistically and realistically nearly impossible for the average person to emulate. There's no way an average American citizen can ever compete with the resources and other elements of materialistic society that these people bring to the table. It would be nice to think that these high standards are there to inspire, but they aren't and they don't.

This constant barrage of unrealistic standards and the everyday American's attempt to attain it only leads to discontentment, low self-esteem, and the feeling of constantly falling short or failing. We are raising kids in an environment where they are bombarded with social media, TV, movies, Netflix, and YouTube and see people doing things and looking ways that they can't ever live up to or match. While it's all a facade, a big game of professional fakery, you have a whole generation of kids who think less of themselves than they should because they are trying to measure up to an impossible standard.

Secondly, celebrities are a poor choice because they are almost always surrounded by people who blow smoke up their ass on the regular and tell them what they want to hear constantly. That means that their thoughts and opinions don't have to be tested and proven in the real world. If they want to help a cause or espouse a particular belief, no one is going to stop them. Of course they are going to speak passionately and with conviction about their beliefs. Of course, they will state their beliefs and opinions with total certainty that makes you feel like they know what the fuck they are talking about. They haven't had their thoughts challenged because they are surrounded by a bunch of highly paid yes-men. And they don't have to think about how their political beliefs translate in *the real world*.

Third, I believe that oftentimes a celebrity's desire to be involved in political issues, social justice, and various other causes is born out of a desire to bring legitimacy to their lives. Deep down, I think many actors and entertainers realize that they pretend for a living and want to stand behind a cause, nonprofit, or political quest to give their lives some additional sense of purpose. This deep need draws celebrities like a magnet to political issues. And, because of their fame and influence, politicians are all too happy to use them as a piece in their political game.

In reality these two should *never* mix. Just because someone can make out with a costar on television in a way that makes your heart flutter or pull off a heart-pounding action sequence in a movie *doesn't qualify them in any way* to speak with authority on political issues or to influence the general population on what we should believe. Most celebrities live in a bubble of fame and wealth that is so far removed from the average person that they have no grasp or concept of how the policies they support will affect everyday people. They feel passion and excitement at the idea of being a part of something real, something that matters, and jump into whatever outlet they can find that will fill that desire. It's their life and they are free to live it however they want. I love a good television show, sports program, and appreciate a good comedian like the next person. I have no problem with celebrities donating to things they care about or taking interest in politics. *But our society must cease to be influenced by their whims or place them in a position of power that they are not qualified to hold.*

One of the unintended consequences of COVID-19 is that it hit the reset button in a hard and brutally honest way as to what is truly important and not to our nation. For those first few weeks of uncertainty as the pandemic spread, actors, professional athletes, and musicians were all but forgotten. No one gave a flying fuck what celebrities were wearing or doing or saying. Without movies in the theaters, sports on television, and concerts, it became rapidly apparent that celebrities do not provide an essential contribution to our nation's well-being. Again, there's nothing inherently wrong with entertainment or those who provide it. Music, movies, and sports are all pleasurable parts of life. We are fortunate to live in a society where we actually have the luxury to idolize actors and athletes. Historically, the idea of investing the amount of time, money, and resources we do into the entertainment industry would have been laughable. People used to be focused on putting food on the table and basic survival. Entertainment is a luxury and privilege and one that is fine to enjoy. We can even appreciate those who provide us with it. But we cannot look to these individuals to influence our views on real life and important political issues.

The bottom line is that celebrities are talented performers. And that's it. Many of them are famous simply for the sake of being famous—without any real skill set. People who produce nothing that our society hinges on for its survivability should not hold the kind of weight they do. Their opinions shouldn't hold any more importance just because they're famous. Their proficiency at their job of pretending for a living does not make their opinion any more valid than yours or mine. If anything, their removal from the plight of the everyday citizen should make their opinion *less* valid. *When we cease to use high levels of competency in **more than one area** as a barometer for who we should look up to and emulate, we become a country that idolizes idiots.*

POLITICIANS

The second type of celebrity that I would identify as a major influence in our society is politicians. Though the president and upper-level cabinet members have always been prominent figures throughout our nation's history, the celebritizing of politicians and government officials is something relatively recent. This is primarily due to the rise of television and social media.

The original purpose of politicians and government officials was to *serve* and *represent* the American people. Over time, however, there has been a reversal of roles. Instead of politicians serving and representing the beliefs and wishes of the people, the people seem to reflect the beliefs of the politicians and serve his or her agenda. The celebritizing of politicians has played a major role in this shift. Nowadays, politicians have social media profiles, extensive funding, and, similar to celebrities, *live lives that are far removed from the lives of everyday Americans.*

You have politicians who work in DC and yet live somewhere else. They have businesses that are largely successful because of the political connections they make. They don't have to worry about money or where their next paycheck is coming from. They get paid handsomely whether they do their fucking job or not. They just need to win the popularity contest and do enough to keep it up. *In many ways they are also highly paid pretenders.* Like actors, they tell people what they want to hear in order to get elected. Once that's out of the way, it's all about getting reelected. Two weeks after taking office, their focus is more about trying to secure their spot the next time around than doing much of anything to actually serve and represent the citizens who elected them in the first place.

There is so much corruption in the American political game we see today. It's filled with backroom deals, personal attacks, cutthroat competitions for popularity, and unforgivable amounts of money. It's embarrassing.

And it's not going to change easily or quickly. Opposing sides calling out each other's bullshit won't work. We need to change the very basis of our entire election process. The only real solution I see to accomplish this is to elect qualified people in much the same way that certain counties choose grand juries by serving papers and requiring the person nominated by most people to fulfill their civic duty and serve on the jury. Here's how this could translate into the election process:

People from a particular region would nominate a fellow citizen from that region whom they deem qualified to serve and represent their interest. Not just anyone could cast a vote to nominate someone. As in the process of choosing a grand jury, only citizens who check a certain list of qualifications are eligible to nominate others. Those qualifications include things like having lived in the area for a certain amount of time, paid taxes in that region for a certain amount of time, not been on welfare, not arrested, etc. This list would simply ensure that they are a productive, contributing member of society who has a vested interest in how tax dollars are spent that isn't biased.

Those qualified individuals would be asked to submit a handful of names as choices for congressman, senator, etc. and the election would be conducted just like any other vote. The person with the most votes would serve and represent that area. Not only would this work to ensure that the right people take office, it would also completely abolish campaign finance corruption. Because there wouldn't be any campaigns. No lobbyists. No backroom deals to secure campaign financing. No wasting thousands of dollars to win the popularity contest. Think of the billions of dollars we could save just by eliminating campaign finance. It's incredible.

Being a politician should not be synonymous with flashy fame, under-the-table deals, and lying for the sake of being popular. It shouldn't be a fight for a moment in the spotlight or a battle for who has more money to invest in campaigning. It should *only* be about qualified people serving and representing their fellow countrymen.

We desperately need capable, upstanding citizens who aren't power and fame hungry to step up to the plate and run for office or play a role in changing the election process to mirror something like I outlined above. Even the average citizen could start a petition for election process change. At the very least, anyone can vote for the right candidate. Not the lesser of two evils, not the person who just isn't the *other* person that you hate, but actually the *right* person. If everyone would do that, change would be made. If everyone decided to either vote for the person they felt was right for the job or not vote at all, we'd be able to get somewhere.

We can't expect real change to happen until individuals remove themselves from the fame game, think independently, and begin to vote with their wallet. It comes down to everyday people like you and me being more selective about where we spend our time and money. It comes down to us changing the way we relate to actors, musicians, and professional athletes. Be selective about where you go for entertainment, make thoughtful choices as to what movies you go and see, TV shows you stream, and celebrity statuses you like or share on social media. That's the best way to send a message. People can't be famous or influential without the masses.

We have to stop allowing ourselves to be spoon-fed. We have to stop allowing celebrities to dictate what we care about, what we hashtag, and how we vote. We have to say enough is enough. We have to stop being dribbling idiots like the sad human blobs in *The Matrix* and start thinking and researching for ourselves. We've become apathetic and unwilling to stand for anything that requires us the least bit of discomfort or sacrifice. And that has to stop.

On the Fourth of July every year, Americans light fireworks, rent a boat on the lake, crack a few beers open, roast some hot dogs, and give a toast to the fact that we live in the good ol' USA. But I think few people take the time to really think about the fifty-six men who put their name on the Declaration of Independence and what they risked to do so. Few people even know the atrocities and hardships that many of them suffered after that document was signed. We overly romanticize our Founding Fathers and don't talk enough about the gritty, harsh realities that they faced and endured on behalf of this country.

The Declaration of Independence is often the high point of our quick history lesson, but seldom do we talk about what happened to those men as a result of their decision to pen those words. Five signers were captured by the British as traitors and brutally tortured and killed. Twelve had their homes ransacked and burned to the ground. Two lost their sons in the revolutionary army, another had two sons taken prisoner. Nine of the fifty-six fought in the Revolutionary War and died from wounds or hardship because of it. One of the men was a wealthy planter and trader and yet was forced to sell his home and properties to pay his debts and died in rags. Another was stalked constantly by the British and forced to move his family repeatedly. He served in Congress without pay and his family was kept in hiding. His possessions were taken from him, and poverty was the gratitude he was paid for his actions.

Another had his home and properties destroyed and the enemy jailed his wife, who died within a few months. Another was driven from his wife's bedside as she was dying. Their thirteen children fled for their lives. His farmland and gristmill were laid to waste and for more than a year he lived in forests and caves. When he returned home, he found his wife dead and his children had vanished. He died just a few weeks later from a shattered heart and exhausted body. Many saw their properties looted by vandals or soldiers or both.

Our country was birthed through great labor pains and sacrifice. The fact that American citizens today possess so little conviction is alarming. The fact that we must be told what to care about and spoon-fed by flashy celebrities and the fact that we are so easily led and influenced—ready to jump on the bandwagon that appears to be the most popular or headed down the path of least resistance—is mind-boggling. It is maddening and it is incredibly sad.

So few people are willing to get outside their comfort zone. So few have the audacity to stand up for anything unpopular. So few are willing to make any personal investment or sacrifice for their country. *It's a luxury, an absolute fucking luxury even, to be afforded the opportunity **not** to care or to choose **not** to get involved, to be okay with mediocrity.* And that's one of our society's greatest downfalls. We've become so successful, fat, and happy that we can afford to be apathetic. But, just as we talked about in the first chapter, that period of riding on the coattails of our nation's previous success has an expiration date. It won't last forever. At some point we have to step up to the plate or we will be forced to in a way that none of us desires.

Is the answer to not have celebrities at all? Is the answer to place no one in high regard? I don't think so. I think it's human nature to want someone to look up to and emulate. I think that our society wants to uphold and reward virtuous people. Just look at the way people go crazy for stories of average people doing something selfless. Someone returns a bag of money or risks their own safety to save someone who's drowning or takes time to walk a little old lady across the street and people go nuts. These stories go viral and you see GoFundMe accounts created for everyday heroes and thousands of dollars are raised on behalf of this type of kindness and sacrifice. This should show us how much our society, at its core, wants to look up to people. Unfortunately, between the media that focuses constantly on the bad and the ugly, and our nation's infatuation with celebrities, we don't see enough examples of good people doing good things and being recognized and rewarded for it.

But that can change. We can start recognizing, rewarding, and supporting our everyday fellow citizens who are doing good things. We can choose to share, promote, and shine light on people who actually deserve the spotlight. Because it's people like that who will inspire the next generation. Instead of upholding unrealistic standards of fake perfection or spotlighting those who pretend for a living, we can choose to uplift those who exemplify common people accomplishing uncommon good.

This change, again, starts with us. We must strive to wake up every day and be the common person who chooses to do uncommon good. We won't be perfect. We will make mistakes. But we are faced with thousands of micro decisions a day and we have the ability to choose right over wrong. So do the right fucking thing, even when no one is looking. Don't just choose the fun, easy thing. Choose the hard, necessary thing. Spotlight, commend, and uphold others who do the same. If and when you get the chance to place someone in front of a camera or on the cover of a magazine or in a position of power, let it be the right person. Vote for them. Tell others about them and share their content on social media. Rather than promoting celebrity gossip or fringe sporting events, bring good people and worthy acts into the spotlight.

Time is the most precious commodity that we are given. The people that you allow to take up your time should be individuals who are worthy of it. Keep your circle of people small and your standards high. The people that I allow into my life and into my daughters' lives are people that I would want to raise my children if I died. That's a good barometer for measuring who you should invest a large amount of your time with and who you shouldn't. If you don't have kids, imagine that you do and ask yourself if the individual you are giving your precious gift of time to is someone you could see raising your future children.

Be selective and intentional on who you spend your time with, both in person and on social media platforms. Surround yourself with people who challenge you and make you better. If everyone were to spend time with people that they want to emulate, the domino effect on society would be inconceivable.

We are all given the choice of how we will spend our time. You get to choose who your friends are, what entertainment you stream on your television, who you follow on social media, what radio, podcasts, or music you listen to in your car, and who you vote for. You choose who you let influence and impact your life and thinking.

People say that "time is money." But I would argue that time is far more valuable than money. You can't produce more of it. You can't pass it on to your kids. You can't save it in a bank account. We've all been given the same finite amount of it. Don't fill your time by default. Don't just let the voices that scream the loudest be the ones that fill your head and influence your thoughts. Don't take the path of least resistance and allow yourself to be spoon-fed. Time is far too limited and far too valuable to be spent like that. And we won't collectively see change in our world until we treat it with the respect it deserves.

CHAPTER 6

*

SHUT UP, KAREN

We're nearing the end of the first section of this book and I hope that the noise and chaos created by our media, celebrity culture, and political environment is quieting down. As much as I'd rather dive right into a discussion on border issues or the economy instead of spending chapters talking about celebrities and social media, I believe that it's imperative that we strip away all blinders and biases before tackling the important issues ahead. Far too many discussions become a tangled web of political agendas, media bias, and supercharged emotions—leaving meager room for any type of productive dialogue.

My hope is that by pulling away and reflecting on the individual strands that created the web we find ourselves in today, we can untangle ourselves and free our minds. We've become so accustomed to having our minds and opinions influenced that it's going to feel pretty goddamn good to have a conversation without anything clouding our judgment.

But, before we get to the next section, there is one more thing I'd like to talk about—a factor in our society that subtly, yet powerfully, interferes with our ability to take positive action and create real change in the areas of our world that need it.

And that factor is virtue signaling and self-righteousness.

The definition of virtue signaling is, *"the action or practice of publicly expressing opinions or sentiments intended to demonstrate one's good character or the moral correctness of one's position on a particular issue."*

The definition of self-righteousness is, *"having or character-ized by a certainty, especially an unfounded one, that one is totally correct or morally superior."*

Read those definitions again. You'd have to live under a fuck-ing rock in Tibet to not see that virtue signaling, coupled with an edge of self-righteous confidence, is running absolutely ram-pant in our society right now. These two elements have woven their gnarly fingers around every important issue of our time— squeezing the life out of anyone who dares to get involved.

Take anything from immigration to racial inequalities to the economy to abortion and you'll find a mob of people posting and arguing about it on social media, holding signs on street cor-ners, writing blog posts and tweets, and everything in between. People preach their position by retweeting information from an "expert" on the subject—filling their news feeds with con-frontational memes, infographics, and stat sheets. They happily take on opposition in the comment sections. It's all done in the name of *"raising awareness"* and *"effecting change"* and *"standing up for what is right."*

But here's the problem.

People have come to mistake the connection and platform that social media provides as a substitute for taking real action and actually creating real change.

This pseudoactivism is detrimental for several reasons. First of all, it is highly ineffective for the most part. We've all scrolled through Facebook before and stumbled upon a heated comment section debate and stayed to watch it unfold. Like the crowds that used to gather in the town square to witness a face-off, we sit back and watch as one person fires off a comment—stating their position and calling into question their opponent's intelligence and basic humanity because they dare to disagree. The other person is quick to come back with their opposing point of view wrapped in *"shame on you, you piece of shit,"* kind of insults. On and on it goes while the rest of us watch silently on our couch in our underwear, waiting to see how it will end.

In reality, we all know how it will end.

Have you ever seen one of those comment battles end with someone saying, "This was an excellent, stimulating conversation and it's given me a lot to think about. This has actually caused me to change my mind on this issue."?

Yeah, me neither.

More often than not, the people who already agree with what you're saying, posting, and tweeting will give you the like, thumbs-up, or supportive comment and the people who don't agree aren't going to change their mind because of your woke hashtag and status. People do not change unless *they see the truth for themselves.* No amount of pushing, prodding, and shaming will do it.

This whole world of social media comment battles, infographic sharing, politically charged hashtags, and "awareness" Instagram challenges show virtue signaling at its finest. Not only is it ineffective, it's actually counterproductive. When people realize that their portfolio of "informed" posts and tweets aren't doing a goddamn thing, they feel the need to up the ante and take it upon themselves to police others and set them straight. It creates a charged environment in which people become more convinced of their own opinions and agitated and enraged by those who disagree. The more this continues, the more compelled they feel to tell others why they are wrong.

The entire definition of virtue signaling revolves around an individual's desire to display their own good character and the moral correctness of their position on a particular issue. Many people today are searching for a sense of purpose. They want to feel like they are *"fighting the good fight," "making a difference in the world,"* and *"creating change."* Social media already provides the opportunity to make a "vacation brochure" out of your life—snapshots of your finest moments and successes. This translates into the whole idea of virtue signaling. People want others to know how socially progressive, forward-thinking, smart, informed, and "woke" they are and they use their personal brochure, a.k.a. social media and other platforms, to demonstrate that.

God forbid that we take time to self-assess and find ways
to productively contribute, take action, or offer our time and
resources to *actually* effect change when it's so much easier to
troll comment sections and set other people straight or repost a
quote or statistic on our Instagram stories.

Far too many important issues are completely overrun by a
flood of people ready to jump at the opportunity to show how
informed and progressive they are by the things they tweet,
share, and post. They're just waiting to flex their "woke" mus-
cles and will leap at any chance to do so.

They want to show how compassionate they are by posting
a heartbreaking picture and statistic on whatever travesty the
world is obsessed with for the week. They want to demonstrate
how brave they are to *"take a stand"* by calling out their Facebook
acquaintances in comment sections when they see the opportunity to have a public disagreement.

We've turned into a world of Karens.

If you've never heard that expression, take a minute and close
your eyes. Imagine a middle-aged woman with shoulder-length
blonde hair whose life's mission is to set other people straight.
She is the neighbor who forms committees and is up everybody's
ass about every tree shrub that isn't cut perfectly. She's the dis-
gruntled diner who wants to speak with the manager. She's the
mom who's constantly telling all the other moms how their kids
are going to die because they vaccinated them or didn't buy the
right brand of cereal. She's the one who is always armed with
an arsenal of "helpful" facts and statistics—awaiting the perfect moment to confront your choices and provide you with a

running list of ways you should improve your life. We've all met a Karen in our life, whether she was our next-door neighbor, our teacher, or the person in front of us at the grocery store. You can't tell me that you don't know the type. It perfectly personifies what our society has become. There are Karens everywhere these days. They are men, women, young, old, gay, straight, and of every political affiliation. And by the way, if your name is Karen and you're offended...guess what? Nobody cares.

Some Karens come in the form of being eco-conscious, planet-saving, fair-trade-coffee-drinking, vegan, social equality experts. Some Karens come in the form of being antigovernment, big-ass-truck-with-a-Trump-bumper-sticker-driving, red-beef-eating, Fox News–lovin' conservatives. There are Karens for nutritional plans and diets, exercise regimens, causes, parenting practices, politics, you name it. Everyone seems to have an inner Karen in them these days.

The truth is that it is a luxury that we even have *the time* to sit around and think about other people's lives as much as we do. It's a luxury that we've evolved so much as a species, and we've made our lives so efficient and optimized that we actually have time to go on social media and shout our beliefs, give out unsolicited information and confrontation, and monitor the opinions of others. Simply put, we're bored. We lack purpose. In many ways, we're a victim of our own successes. And so we chase any platform or soapbox available to sit above the rest of humanity and point fingers.

Imagine if we added up all the hours that people spend on social media policing others and posting about things they are supposedly passionate about. Imagine if we dedicated that same amount of time to volunteer work and other actionable contributions to the causes that people supposedly champion. We might actually see real change take place.

To me, virtue signaling is the epitome of an entitled attitude. What makes us think that we are so much better than everyone else? What gives us the audacious arrogance to assume that we can rightly judge the political viewpoint of someone that we've never even met based on a social media post?

While writing this book, I witnessed virtue signaling in full swing both surrounding the spread of COVID-19 and the Black Lives Matter movement. People fought in comment sections over whether or not they should have to wear a mask in public, how many people were dying, and how people should run their businesses in the face of a pandemic. Just a few weeks later there were massive movements on social media, pressuring people to post a black screen on their profile or add a hashtag to further the Black Lives Matter movement. Even silence was enough to cause people to judge other people, saying that *"silence is violence."* Just a simple refusal to follow the masses seemed to be incriminating proof of racism.

In both the case of COVID-19 and the BLM movement, virtue signaling was on display: *"the action or practice of publicly expressing opinions or sentiments intended to demonstrate one's good character or the moral correctness of one's position on a particular issue."* No one wants to be the one left behind or judged or shamed. The fear of falling behind or being left out creates a herd mentality in which people are quick to follow the crowd when they see enough people doing so. Remember your dad saying, "If your friends jumped off a cliff, would you jump too?" The scary thing is that people today are so heavily influenced by the world of media and so bent on following the crowd that we shouldn't be surprised when the whole fucking herd leaps off the cliff together.

There are those who will argue that they aren't a "Karen," but rather a dedicated soul who simply *informs* and *educates* others on issues that they care about. Unfortunately, with the rise of technology and access to limitless amounts of information, you can find "science" or "expert opinions" or "credible statistics" that back up two completely opposing points of views. Those of us who lived through COVID-19 saw this in action daily. One doctor says the virus isn't that bad. Another says it's leading the masses to an agonizing death. You can find "science" or "facts" supporting a whole range of positions on just about anything.

This means that "informational" posts don't carry much weight at all. I hate to break it to you but posting facts and statistics on social platforms probably isn't doing all that much good. Virtue signaling is the *Reader's Digest/CliffsNotes* version of activism and, without a doubt, a poor substitute for it.

We've covered a variety of negative elements in our current culture through these last several chapters that confuse and inhibit productive conversation and positive change from taking place. With the storm of media and celebrities, virtue signaling, and rapidly changing culture, it's no wonder that we can't seem to get much traction to move forward in the areas our nation needs it in the most. Through the last few chapters we've identified many of the factors that have contributed to the politically and emotionally charged chaos that we see surrounding every important issue today. We need to change how we go about assessing important issues and making up our minds. If we are going to do away with the heavy influence of culture, celebrities, media, and other people, we need to develop a process, as individuals, for making up our own minds about important issues.

I'd like to offer four cornerstone principles that can be used as a guide for assessing and approaching *any* important subject, issue, or problem. If every individual implemented the practice of utilizing these principles, I think we'd see a lot change. It's a four-step process and here's how it works:

1. Remove emotions
2. Remove politics
3. Mind your own fucking business
4. Hold yourself to the same or higher standard that you hold others to

That's it.

When you first look at an issue, start by removing emotion. If you are angry, offended, distressed, pessimistic, charged up, or overly empathetic, you'll never be able to assess it logically. That's why emotion must be removed first.

Secondly, remove politics. It's *vital* to remove any preconceived ideas and political biases that you have before you assess an issue or dialogue about it. If you come in with your

Democratic or Republican or whatever party glasses on, you're never going to be able to see or discuss any issue clearly.

Third, take your attention away from policing everyone around you and instead focus on your own life and your own actions by minding your own fucking business. This practice alone would clear away so much chaos in our world today. None of us is entitled to judge another human being. Unless an individual is causing harm to his fellow man in some way, (and no, your precious feelings being hurt does *not* constitute actual harm) we would all do well to generally leave people the fuck alone, let them conduct their lives the way they see fit, and spend our time worrying about ourselves.

Lastly, hold yourself accountable to *at least the same standard* you hold everyone else to. Again, if everyone did this we'd finally see some real change happen. If we didn't lie to ourselves when we fuck up, if we didn't look for someone to blame, if we allowed others to learn from our mistakes, if we were willing to point the finger at ourselves instead of others, and if we forced *ourselves* to take action like we push everyone else to, we'd make headway so fucking fast our nation wouldn't know what hit it.

Implementing these four principles is something I strive for on a daily basis. It's how I seek to approach any important issue I come across. It's also what we'll use as a guide and framework for breaking down the topics in the following section. I'll be the first to admit that I'm by no means perfect and am well aware that there are areas in which I fall short on all four of these accounts. But it's helped me tremendously in maintaining independent views and unbiased beliefs.

I promised to be honest and straightforward in this book. If I'm going to call you out, I want to give you a very real example from my own life where I broke all four of the rules I outlined above and own up to my shortcomings.

Many of you remember when San Francisco 49ers quarterback Colin Kaepernick sat and later knelt during the anthem, before his team's preseason games of 2016. Throughout the following seasons, members of various NFL and other sports teams engaged in similar silent protests. The first time I saw this, I was fucking furious. As a Navy SEAL, I have witnessed the bodies of some of the greatest men I know and will ever know being draped in that flag. I have stood alongside hundreds of fellow brothers-in-arms who have been overseas and witnessed untold horrors, watching as one of our very own brothers-in-arms is lowered into the ground with that flag over him. That flag represents the freedom that I and so many others have risked our lives for. So when I witnessed the players' protests, I was enraged. It felt like a slap in the face to me and everyone who had ever put their life on the line for this country. I was ready for something to be done to put a stop to these disrespectful acts.

When it happened, I was so wrapped up in being incredulous, swayed by my own political beliefs, and fueled by a flood of emotions due to my life experience and personal connection to it all that I couldn't clearly assess the situation. What I hadn't realized is that I had broken all four of the principles outlined above. I had allowed both politics and emotions to cloud my judgment. I was not minding my own business, but rather obsessing over the actions of someone I had never met.

And lastly, I wasn't holding my beliefs to the same standard as I hold others to. When I removed my emotions, I forced myself to think logically and recognized that the NFL was, after all, a business. And it is their right to decide whether or not they are going to allow their employees to do what they did in a company uniform on company time.

Though the actions of those players still deeply bother me, I realized that if I were to call for the government to jump in and take action, I'd be a fucking hypocrite. If we are going to be in a society in which we are truly free and have liberty based on a constitutional republic, it has to apply to things that *we don't agree with*, that make us uncomfortable, that we don't like. Whether or not I like it, those men have the right to do what they did. At the end of the day, their actions aren't any of my business. I had to take a hard look in the mirror and see that it would be wrong of me to suddenly adopt a double standard simply because it enraged me and went against my personal political beliefs. It was a tough pill to swallow, but it is vastly important that I hold myself accountable and challenge myself to uphold the freedom I stand for, even in a tough situation.

Virtue signaling, in its essence, is the direct result of refusing to hold yourself accountable. There is a childlike petulance to blaming others and pointing the finger for the problems we see. The busier you are blaming or shaming someone, the less time you have to reflect on your own actions and choices. I don't care who you are or what hand you were dealt in life, all of us have been given opportunity and the choice to do with it what we want.

Some people want to talk about how they've been wronged, victimized, or mistreated and claim it's the cause of their inability to take action. But no matter how bad you have it, how poor your family was, or how abused you were, there are countless stories in our world today and throughout history of someone who had it worse and still made something of themselves. Because they were willing to look internally and ask, "What can I do today to become a better person, improve my situation, and contribute to the world around me?"

We need more people brave enough to ask that question.

I read a quote recently from Andy Frisella that said, "Show me your last 1,000 days and I'll show you why you are exactly where you are in life." Each of us should ask ourselves, "If someone looked at my last one thousand days, what would they see? What have I done to become a better person? How have I meaningfully contributed my time and resources to the issues that I claim I am so passionate about? What do my daily habits look like?"

Change will only begin when we are willing to hold ourselves responsible for our own lives and take meaningful action.

We are going to discuss some pretty weighty matters in the following chapters. I hope that we can do so without pointing fingers and blaming others, without political bias, and without emotion. It's not what is written on these pages that will alter society. The shift comes down to you and me and every other citizen of this country and the daily choices each of us makes.

At the risk of sounding like a broken record because I've said it before, buckle up because you're going to hear it quite a few more times before we're done: the best way that we can change things in our world is to remove our blinders and invest our time and mental energy into honest self-evaluation and taking responsibility for our own choices. We won't get anywhere by shaming others for the way they live their lives, but by setting an example by how we live ours.

CHAPTER 7

★

OUR BORDERS

O
ver the next several chapters, we'll talk about a number of issues and challenges our nation is facing right now. The one I'd like to talk about first is the security of our borders. I want to start there because there are numerous issues that either stem from, or at the very least are incredibly aided by, the lack of security at our borders. The three most significant ones are human trafficking, drug trade, and terrorism. We'll take a deeper look at each of these in the future chapters, but we'll briefly touch on all three here as they pertain to our borders.

HUMAN TRAFFICKING

Human trafficking increases with every passing year. The Polaris Project estimates that there were 22,326 trafficking victims and survivors identified in the United States in 2019. The Trafficking Hotline saw a nearly *20 percent increase* in the number of victims and survivors who contacted them directly about their own situations from 2018–2019. Again, we'll devote an entire chapter to discussing this particular issue, but it's worth bringing up here because it's the lack of security at our border that has provided a massive opening for traffickers.[19]

DRUG TRADE

Drug trade has also skyrocketed in the past ten years. Only a small percentage of illegal drugs are actually found and seized at the border. With drug cartels gaining money and power, they are quickly becoming an invisible, controlling force within our nation. The security at our borders is grossly lacking and there are powerful people who are capitalizing on that fact, using our negligence to their advantage.

TERRORISM

Terrorism is something that remains on the minds of every American since the attacks of 9/11. While we've made some strides to fight terrorism, it is still a very real threat. There are those who wish our nation harm and will exploit any opportunity to do so.

---

19 "2019 US National Human Trafficking Hotline Statistics," *Polaris*, November 12, 2020, https://polarisproject.org/2019-us-national-human-trafficking-hotline-statistics/.

In addition to these three dangerous issues there is also the alarming number of illegal immigrants flooding across the borders without the consent of our government. Despite the wealth of unsettling information surrounding this issue, many are opposed to the idea of increased border security. There are even those who would advocate diminishing it or eradicating it altogether. Border security has become a controversial topic and there is no shortage of high emotions and vehement disagreement surrounding it. That's why I want to spend some time peeling back the bullshit and having a logical conversation about it.

So let's start at the beginning. The idea of borders, walls, and territorial boundaries dates back to the beginning of human inception. Borders define a country, give it shape, and quite literally *put it on the map*. Across the world today, borders and walls still serve the same purpose. They differentiate one territory from another. It's as simple as that. Humans have widely accepted this commonsense approach to sharing this big ball we call Earth for centuries.

However, in recent years, there has been a rising uproar against the idea of maintaining secure borders. There are some who would even go as far as to say that we need to get rid of border security altogether. To me this idea is ludicrous. Without borders, we aren't really a country at all. To adopt this kind of thinking would be the surrender of everything that we, as a nation, have worked so hard to build and protect.

To me, a conversation about our borders should be a simple one. It should be a straightforward, commonsense issue. But in recent years it has morphed into something else entirely. It's now a hot-button topic, filled with high emotion and riddled with political land mines. This is where the cornerstone principles that I outlined in the previous chapter come into play. We're never going to get anywhere unless we remove emotions, remove politics, learn to mind our own fucking business, and hold ourselves to the same standard we hold everyone else to. We'll use these four things as a framework by which we approach this issue and the others that we will discuss in the chapters to come. While breaking it down in this way may seem like an oversimplified process, it is an incredibly effective way to gain clear minds and viable solutions in our chaotic climate.

REMOVE EMOTIONS

Emotions are part of being human. They make you feel warm and fuzzy when you meet someone attractive. They give you the ability to feel someone else's pain sympathetically. They make you teary-eyed when you look through old photographs of your children when they were young. They spring into action when someone cuts in front of you in an intersection. They flood in like a broken dam when you lose someone you love. Emotions are integral to human experience. But here's the thing. *Emotions cloud logical thinking.* Emotions place colored lenses over your eyes and make you see the world in a shaded way.

That's why emotions cannot be the foundation on which laws and legislation are passed and they do not provide a reliable compass for navigating important issues or determining the course of our nation's future. If you want to be angry about your football team losing or tell your husband how you were snubbed at work, let the emotions in. If you want to enjoy a leisurely dinner flirting with a beautiful woman, let 'em fly. If your father is diagnosed with cancer, let the tears out. But if you want to have an important conversation about our nation, if you want to discuss the creation of laws and policy, if you want to form an objective opinion regarding an important political issue, then *they must be removed.*

So let's talk about emotions as it pertains to border security. Undoubtedly, you've scrolled through your social media and come across compelling photography depicting impoverished immigrants and young children wearing shirts with the words "Don't deport my daddy" on them. These images pull at our heartstrings, and thus our emotions. *How could we not help? We have more than enough to go around. How can we not welcome more people into our country? Isn't that what this country was founded on?*

There is a basic desire in all good-hearted, warm-blooded humans to want to help our fellow man. As American citizens, we enjoy a level of freedom and opportunity that not everyone in the world does and there's nothing wrong with extending an invitation to others to enjoy that freedom. But high emotions, and a media that plays to them, lead far too many people to make a quantum leap from a desire to offer others a better life to the idea that we should open our borders completely—come one, come all. People have begun to think that it's our duty to welcome anyone and everyone into our nation. We think that anyone who wants to enforce border security or clearly define the boundaries of our borders is heartless, unfeeling, and cruel.

But again, we cannot create laws and policies based upon emotion. The unfortunate truth is that there is a limited amount of resources available to us in the United States. Just like there are only so many people who can fit in a boat before it sinks or a house before it collapses or eat at Pizza Hut before the pizza runs out, there is a finite number of people who can comfortably live here.

We'd like to think that we have unlimited resources to share with the world, but in truth, we do not. And while we may not be at the limits of our capacity now, take a look at statistics and the rate at which illegal immigration has grown in the past ten years and you'll quickly see that we cannot sustain the path we're on forever and we certainly can't afford to open the barn doors to anyone and everyone. This isn't heartless or cruel. It's simply a fact. When emotions are removed, it comes down to simple math and common sense.

Imagine a mother is sitting with her five children in an airplane and it loses pressure. The oxygen masks drop and she has a choice to make. The impulsive decision would be to begin masking the children. After all, what mother *wouldn't* put her children first? But the truth is that if she does not first put the mask on herself and ensure that she has the necessary oxygen in her own lungs to think and act clearly, she will likely pass out in the process of trying to put masks on the children, ultimately putting herself and those who need her at risk.

This analogy rings true in this instance as well. We'd like to think that our resources—power, water, food, medical supplies and professionals—are unlimited. But there is an ecosystem in place that creates the environment in which we live and if it is overtaxed, it will change. And when the rubber meets the road, I don't think that even the truest believers in the idea of abolishing border security are prepared for living within that reality. We'll discuss that more in just a moment.

REMOVE POLITICS

An excellent example of how political bias clouded the view of Americans on this particular issue can be seen clearly throughout the Trump administration. In fact, "Build a wall!" might be the three words that President Trump was best known for saying. In case you were off the grid in Laos and didn't read headlines or social media during those years, I'll go ahead and tell you that President Donald Trump didn't often win popularity contests in the media. During his presidency, a significant portion of the population seemed to have a broad dislike, even hatred for President Trump. They hated that he was elected, they hated that he was the leader of our nation. They thought he was a bully. They thought he was a terrible human. And this is the lens through which they saw and interpreted every issue he took on.

This is an unfortunate reality when it comes to border issues. The single fact that increasing border security was a primary focus of the Trump administration has been reason enough for many people to adopt a visceral opposition to the entire idea without a second thought. People have allowed their political biases and emotion in the form of anger, hatred, and resentment to completely interfere with sound thought or judgment when it comes to this issue.

These dynamics have long been in play, well before the Trump administration. Far too often, people have the mentality that when the political party opposite their own takes office they should oppose everything they are for. They allow their dislike for the president to inform their position on every issue automatically. If he says yes, they say no. If he says go, they say stop. If he says right, they say wrong.

Here's what I would say to that. If your beliefs and opinions on border issues are tied to what your political party's opinion of the president is, then you're a fucking moron. You don't have to like a guy to agree with him. You don't have to ascribe to his political party or agree with all that he stands for to admit that you actually think he has some valid points.

The political climate has changed a lot in the past few decades. Issues like border security weren't always as emotionally and politically charged as they are today. But, as we discussed in previous chapters, the attacks of 9/11 and the birth of the twenty-four-hour news cycle brought with it a new political landscape. One that is chaotic, polarized, and brimming with confusion. This has created further divisiveness on every single issue we face today.

When a Republican is president, half the nation folds their arms and pouts, disagrees with everything he says, and tries to oppose it at every turn. And when a Democrat is president, the converse takes place. How do we expect to make any traction on important issues when we approach every single goddamn issue predisposed to thinking one way or another based on our like or dislike of the person who is currently president?

It's sad and unfortunate that people have chosen an issue that is relevant to our national security as a way to show their personal disdain for a man they don't like. Sure, people like to claim that it wasn't all about the Trump administration, saying that they just deeply care about the poor and needy of the world. That they just want to show a little human decency and open our borders to the less fortunate. But here's the thing. If you care that much about people who are struggling in the world, why aren't you hopping on a plane and volunteering at refugee camps? Why aren't the rooms of your own house filled with the people you say you want to help so much? To me, it's pathetic to allow your bruised-up feelings over your team losing the presidential race to inform the way you relate to a matter as serious as the security of our borders. Political bias is a powerful thing. And that's why it's imperative that we remove it in order to look at this issue clearly.

MIND YOUR OWN FUCKING BUSINESS

On the issue of border security and immigration, there is a lot of misinformation that flies around. And oftentimes, the people at the very forefront of the discussion have absolutely no business giving their opinion because they have *absolutely no experience in or expertise on* the matter. If you don't have experience on a subject, you are entitled to have an opinion. But that opinion is useless because it's not backed by anything. There is a startling lack of subject matter experts placed in a position to *influence* decision-makers or *be* decision-makers when it comes to border security. Far too many politicians, with no fucking experience whatsoever, are the ones blindly leading the crusade.

We need political leaders who know the limits of their knowledge and know when it's time to bring experienced, proven experts into the decision-making process. We need leaders who are humble enough to stay in their lane and not talk out of their asses about issues that they have no actual experience with. A senator has no business dictating how many beds there should be in a border holding area or how protocol for border security is put into action. I want to look at them and say, "Sorry, motherfucker, but you haven't worked a shift arresting people on the border a day in your life and you're going to tell people who've spent decades doing just that how to do their job? On what arrogant goddamn planet do you live that you think you have a better understanding of the intricacies involved in this issue than they do? You think that just because you flew down and spent three hours on the border snapping photos with your six aides surrounding you that you have a pulse on the complexities of the situation? Fuck off. I think not."

We need to have people in positions of power within our government who know the bounds of their expertise and stay within it or do the work to expand it. I'm not saying we don't need politicians and government officials. We do. But good leaders should know the limits of their expertise and experience. They should know how to assemble the right team to solve problems and execute solutions. They should do a much better job of listening to the people who have their boots on the ground.

HOLD YOURSELF TO THE SAME STANDARD
YOU HOLD EVERYONE ELSE TO

If there is a big-picture policy that you think is a good idea, I'd suggest the following as a litmus test. It's a great way to analyze your thinking and see if the logic behind it holds. It isn't hard and doesn't cost you anything but a little intellectual flexibility.

Here's how it works. Take your big-picture policy and reduce it to a specific micro decision that you could implement in your own life that would mirror your position. You could use a belief or opinion you hold about our nation (the macro view) and compare it on a much smaller scale to your state, your city, or your own home (the micro view) and then test your beliefs accordingly. Would you be willing to implement *your* position in *your own life*?

Let's apply this macro/micro test to the issue at hand. Let's say that you believe that we should reduce or abolish border security and open our borders to welcome in anyone and everyone. That's your belief on a large scale, macro level. So let's test your position on a micro level. Would you leave your door unlocked at night so that anyone who needed your resources could come in and help themselves at will? Are you ready to tear down your backyard fence and let it be the community hub for every neighbor to use it as they see fit? Would you be willing to open your doors and allow unlimited immigrants and refugees to come into your home, even if it meant that your own children went hungry?

The truth is that few people who advocate abolishing border security and claim they want to welcome people from all corners of the earth with open arms would actually be willing to give up their comfort, their freedom, and their way of life.

To the people who want to stand on a pedestal and preach their anti-border ideas while living in a gated community with high security and locks on their doors at night, basking in the glow of their little piece of untouched American paradise, I have one thing to say:

Fuck you.

No seriously, fuck you.

You are a hypocrite and a thief. You want other people to spend money, other people to make the sacrifices to carry out your kumbaya-let's-invite-everyone-in agenda while you pat yourself on the back and congratulate yourself on how "empathetic" and "compassionate" you are. I have no use for these types of double standards, especially in policy makers and those in positions of power, to make real-world decisions. Nothing chaps my ass more than the fact that there are numerous anti-gun, anti-wall senators who leave their offices and drive their shiny sports cars over to their gated communities that are protected by armed guards, inside the most pristine area of town, and they sit back at the end of the day and have a glass of wine, feeling like such a little world changer while their entire life is a total, hypocritical contradiction.

If you're not willing to live by the same standard that you advocate everyone else living, then again:

Fuck you.

While I am obviously passionate about hypocrisy, especially when exhibited by our leaders who are in a position of power,

I truly believe that there are many people who simply haven't considered the logical end to the positions they ascribe to. Influenced by emotions and politics, they hear a large-scale solution like reducing border security and think, "Yeah! That sounds like a good idea." without considering the real implications of it. Many people haven't followed their sympathetic plan to its logical end.

To those people, I would encourage honestly applying the macro/micro litmus test. Take your beliefs and see if they hold up in real life, in your own life. Far too often people are divorced from the reality of what their beliefs, if carried out, will *actually mean*. As someone who has come nose to nose with the sacrifice it takes to protect this nation and who's been the literal boots on the ground to carry out orders from people in high places, I think it's vastly important that every citizen test their thinking and ask themselves if they would be willing to handle the implications of it.

Because someone, somewhere will have to face the reality of your position if put in action.

It's easy to stand for something on social media, hold a sign and march around a town square, cast a vote, and then return to your happy, safe, air-conditioned bubble without ever having to feel the consequences and implications of your position. I have numerous friends who work tirelessly at our borders for the sole purpose of ensuring our safety and way of life. It's not an easy task. The sad thing is that many people want to demonize these men and vote against policies that would assist them in their difficult jobs just because they hate the golden-haired man in office or read an article about immigrants who pulled at their heartstrings. And, all the while, they never think twice about all the ways they are benefiting from the safety provided by our border security.

This is why there is incredible power in applying the four principles to any issue. We've removed emotions. We've removed political bias. We've made sure that we're minding our own business and not pretending to be experts on subjects that we lack experience in. We've tested our thinking to see if we are holding ourselves to the same standard that we hold everyone else to.

With emotions, political bias, and incongruous beliefs removed, finding solutions for this issue will be a challenge, but the path is definitely a little clearer. The magnitude of this problem is hard to fathom and can even seem too daunting to know where to begin. But we have to try. We can't just keep kicking the can down the road and hope that it will go away. When Japan attacked Pearl Harbor and the American people sat and watched as a depraved German dictator took over country after country in his quest to rule the world, it seemed that finding a path to victory was an insurmountable task. But we rolled up our sleeves, came together, and we found a way. That resilient attitude is what makes this country great. And no, dipshit, I'm not equating illegal immigrants to Nazis. Simmer down. I'm simply saying that we can't sit on our hands and not try to address the problem.

I'd like to offer a few of my own personal thoughts and opinions on solutions for change as well as actionable things that the average person can do in regard to this topic.

START WITH SECURING OUR BORDERS
AND SECURING THEM WELL

Imagine for a moment that your toilet is overflowing. Water is gushing out of it, seeping all over your carpet. What are you going to do first? Are you going to grab a mop and try to absorb the water while it continues to gush? Or are you going to shut off the water and then deal with the flood?

Trying to address the problem of what to do with the people who are illegally already within our borders without first securing the border is akin to grabbing a mop and trying to mop up the water spouting out of the toilet while it continues to overflow. It doesn't make sense. The leak needs to be fixed first. Then the mess can be cleaned up. There are way too many people watching the overflowing toilet saying, "Even if we start mopping the floor now, we'll never get it clean. There's too much water pouring out!" And if you aren't going to stop the flood, you're right. No amount of mopping will fix the problem. But if you stop the flow and fix the leak first, cleaning up the mess might be a big task, but it certainly won't be impossible.

And again, if you're getting all butt-ass hurt because you think I'm equating people to toilet water, you can choke yourself. It's a fucking analogy, not some deep parallel. Just follow the logic. My point is that the borders need to be secured first and foremost and they need to be secured well. We need to have full control over who is coming inside our borders so that we can ensure the safety and well-being of US citizens.

How do we do this?

Find Subject Matter Experts and
Place Them in a Position of Power

The single greatest thing that we can do to solve the complex issues of border security is to pull together people who are subject matter experts on all aspects of this topic and sit our asses down and actually *listen* to their thoughts, ideas, needs, and solutions. And then actually *do* something with that information.

In this case, as with many others, there are people making decisions on a high level without intimate knowledge of the tactical, boots-on-the-ground aspects of the situation. They are looking at it from an operational standpoint—the "30,000 feet view," the big picture overview. While this is a necessary perspective, it's not the only perspective that's needed. When you only see the 30,000 feet, operational view, without the tactical, boots-on-the-ground understanding of how your marching orders are actually going to translate, you run into problems. I could give you countless examples from my experience serving as a Navy SEAL of this very problem in action. *Large, operational decisions must be influenced by the people who handle the day-to-day, tactical aspects of the issue at hand.*

Unfortunately, law and policy makers are primarily influenced by political undercurrents and people who have absolutely nothing to do with the actual issue. Again, I've seen these dynamics play out countless times in the military. *When leaders make decisions based upon what they think is the most politically expedient choice at the time, people get killed. It simply doesn't work.*

We need to eliminate this disconnect by bringing in people with an operational perspective along with those who have tactical experience. We need to allow subject matter experts to inform our decisions and policies. People who've never spent a day patrolling the border shouldn't be the only ones deciding the rules of engagement. We need to hear from people whose job it is to carry out the master plan when they come in for work on Monday. We need to listen to what they need and give them the resources to do their jobs well. If we did this one simple thing we'd see a tremendous breakthrough in effectiveness in maintaining secure borders.

Utilize In-Country Refugee Camps

So what about refugees? This is a common question when issues concerning our borders arise. The most successful solutions to refugee crises around the world have come when temporary camps are set up *in the refugees' country of origin* to aid in protecting them in the midst of war or natural disaster. These camps can provide temporary shelter until the imminent danger has passed and then resources can be invested to help them rebuild what was lost.

Not all refugees need to leave their country. It might seem like the easiest solution in the short term, but it can create many long-term problems. If a dangerous situation arises that puts a group of people at risk in a particular location, it would be much better if they were to temporarily relocate within their own borders and then return to restore and rebuild when the danger has passed. This model has been shown to be very effective. It is also a much better use of the funds that would be tied up trying to hold and process asylum seekers in the United States.

Create Incentives and Enforce Consequences

While this might sound like a simple concept, if we created increased incentives for people going through the proper channels to become a US citizen and consequences for coming into our country the wrong way and then stood behind both without exception, it would help the situation tremendously. Unfortunately, we don't have much in the way of incentives or consequences. People have very little reason to *want* to do the right thing and very little reason to avoid doing the wrong thing. Should we be surprised that this problem has gotten so out of hand?

Place a Premium on the Integration of New Citizens into Our Culture

Our country was founded upon the blending of different cultures—people from various parts of the world coming together and contributing to the building of a new society. Many people bring up this fact in conversations on border security and immigration.

It is true, our nation was founded on the backs of immigrants who came to this territory with the hope of a better life. If you were an able-bodied person with a skill, a dream, and a desire to pitch in and help to build a new society, you were welcome. In the beginning we had a vast territory and very few people inhabiting it by comparison. Limited people meant limited skill sets. We needed doctors, blacksmiths, farmers, teachers, and many others to create a well-rounded, robust society.

Look at the family unit at that time in history and you'll see that most people had seven or more children. Why? It was an all-hands-on-deck situation. People needed the extra hands, needed to bolster society with the extra humans, so they produced as many as possible. Look at the family unit today and you'll see that most people have on average 1.9 children per family. This is another example of how looking at the micro view (the family unit) can help us better understand the macro view (our nation at large). Times have obviously changed quite a bit since the beginning of our nation. At one point in time, we needed as many able bodies with varying skill sets as possible because our American culture and society hadn't yet formed. Since then, we have successfully built a strong, unique American culture and society and we aren't desperate for more people to fill our land.

That's why it's important to assess each individual seeking US citizenship and ask what they bring to the table. How can they better our society? What skills do they offer? What do they have to add and contribute? This is something that Australia exemplifies very well in their process of granting citizenship. Of course, there are cases in which we grant asylum or citizenship to those who have very little, but in many cases, it would be advantageous for us to see what the individual seeking citizenship can contribute to our society.

Additionally, I think it's very important for those who make the decision to become American citizens to integrate into American society and culture. There is a high premium placed on diversity and honoring other cultures in the United States today. And while there are certainly many wonderful things that people can bring to the table from a variety of unique backgrounds, the first priority of anyone who becomes an American citizen should be learning our language, culture, customs, and way of life.

When someone has enough incentive to go to the trouble to leave their country of origin and become an American citizen, the majority of the time it's due to the fact that they did not feel safe in their country, didn't have enough opportunity, or experienced some difficulty. To me, if that's the case, it doesn't make a lot of sense that they would then turn around and try to make America more like the country they left once they are here. As a side note, this could also be applied to US citizens moving from one state to another. If you move from California to Texas, don't try to make Texas like California. And vice versa. If you wanted to live within the context and culture you were born into, you could have stayed. The same is true with immigration. If you want to live within the American context and culture, then dive in and be a part of what our country has to offer. I would never expect to move to another country and presume that they should change their culture to fit mine. I would see it as my job to do everything I could to integrate into *their* culture and become a contributing member of *their* society.

I think that learning English and taking the basic citizen test are sufficient requirements for becoming a citizen. On this point, I'd also add that I believe that every high school student should be required to pass the citizenship test before graduation. Sadly, I guarantee you that 90 percent of our high school graduates would fail it. It's important that we uphold the same standard as citizens that we require of those who come into our nation.

As with every subject we cover, I want to end by bringing our conversation back to what you and I can do to take action in our personal lives and play our part to help in the midst of challenges we face. Here are a few things that anyone can do in regard to this issue.

EDUCATE YOURSELF

First and foremost, I think it's important to educate yourself on the issues. Do what you need to do to be informed and don't shy away from the problem or try to sugarcoat it because it's daunting and scary. More people need to understand the magnitude of the problem we're facing here, they need to know statistics on human trafficking and drug trade, and they need to put some thought into what the future will look like if we don't address these issues. Be humble enough to admit that there is a problem. Be brave enough to listen to people you don't like if they have valid thoughts and solutions.

All of us should remain vigilant in removing our political blinders and personal feelings about those in office and trade them for logical, clear-headed thinking and action. Take time to research the issues that we've discussed, along with others. And fulfill your duty as an American citizen and vote with a clear and independent mind.

DON'T BE GASOLINE ON A FOREST FIRE

Another thing that you can do, no matter who you are, is to refuse to be another person adding fuel to the political and emotional flame surrounding this issue. Don't be another person who cares more about insulting their president than protecting their nation. Don't be another person who skim reads one article and thinks they're an expert. We're so busy fighting with one another that our country is slipping away from us. I'm not an expert on the ins and outs of border issues and neither are you. What we *can do* is find ways to spotlight and lift up the people who are actually out there working, day in and day out, to protect our borders and we can refuse to perpetuate more chaos, confusion, and misinformation on the subject.

I have intentionally kept my opinions on this subject broad because I truly believe that we would do best to listen to the opinions of those with experience and expertise. I can tell you with certainty that we have a problem and offer my thoughts as a framework for assessing the issue. But I'm not offering specific recommendations and solutions here because it's my belief that we need to be listening to subject matter experts and let them lead the conversation on the implementation of specific solutions. I do want to be clear that I *am for immigration*. Though I've spent the majority of this chapter talking about the problems and issues we face due to lack of border security and regulations, I absolutely believe that we should continue to extend the opportunity to others to live here. I love this beautiful place I call home and want to be able to share that with others.

In closing, there is one last thing that I would like to say.

Evil does exist in this world. I love the idea that every person's desire for coming inside our borders is rooted in simply wanting a better life. But it's just not true. While this is often the case, the unfortunate reality is that there are others who wish harm on this country and would love nothing more than to take advantage of our kindness to hurt and terrorize our citizens.

If we don't keep a pulse on who is coming in and out of our country, if we don't put a force in place to regulate it, we will continue to be left in the dark on who we are allowing in. Would you knowingly leave your doors unlocked at night and listen to the footsteps of strangers walk your halls and enter your children's rooms and not even bother to check who it is? Would you lay there and think, "They're probably just here because they need to borrow something" or "I'm sure it's a good person"?

There are forces of evil in this world that are powerful. And until you've actually stared evil in the face and been forced to confront it with your own life, it's easy to pretend as though it doesn't exist. As someone who has come nose to nose with forces in this world that wish our nation harm, I can tell you that this naivety will come at a great cost.

We cannot afford to give up or simply turn a blind eye.

We cannot afford the luxury of naivety.

We may have a long road ahead but our nation has never backed down from a challenge and we're damn sure not going to start now.

CHAPTER 8

✳

AMERICA'S INEQUALITIES

Since the birth of our nation, the story of America has been one of resilience, independence, human ingenuity, and courage. But there are many parts of that story that are far from perfect. The very freedom and equality that our country was founded upon did not always extend to all people. There was a time when women were not allowed to vote or have the same rights as men. There was a time when it was legal to own and enslave other human beings. There was a time when no one thought twice about sorting and segregating people based upon their skin color.

These oppressive acts committed by citizens of our nation are egregious. They are inexcusable. They fly in the face of everything our country stands for. Those chapters in our history are dark ones. Ones that all of us, if given the chance, would erase if we could.

In the last hundred years, we've made massive strides in ridding our nation of oppression and inequality in our laws, policies, and society at large. In 1920, women were given the right to vote. In the following years, laws and policies were passed to ensure equality for women not only in politics, but also in the workplace and all other areas. As the father of two strong, independent daughters, I am grateful for the opportunities available to them that women for centuries did not have.

In addition, the segregation of facilities, services, and opportunities such as housing, medical care, education, employment, and transportation in the United States along racial lines was put to an end and changes were made in all aspects of life to ensure equality and representation for people of color. It's hard for me to even wrap my mind around the fact that there was a day when this kind of inhumane treatment was acceptable, a day when some of my dearest friends would not have been able to sit with me at a restaurant or put their children in the same school as mine simply because of their skin color.

These corrections were necessary. They were long overdue. And the changes that have stemmed from them are very apparent in our world today. Women, people of color, and almost all minority groups are now represented in all positions of power—in business, politics, entertainment, and government.

It's incredible to see how far we've come. In the 1960s, would you have seen a Black Supreme Court justice? Would you have seen a Black president? No. Would you have seen numerous powerful female CEOs? Unlikely. Would you have seen a Black, female police chief in Dallas, Texas? Fuck no. Today, you can see all of those. This is tangible evidence that the measures we have put into place to ensure equal opportunity have succeeded and are succeeding. It is now possible for anyone to achieve all of the things that were once only available to White, straight men—from being an astronaut to a CEO to a judge to the president of the United States. It's beautiful.

Having said all of this, we need to talk about the *trajectory* of where our nation is headed in regards to this issue. I know I am treading into a sensitive topic here. I am also aware that I am talking about this issue as a White, straight, middle-class male. Even still, I am wading into the waters because it is vital that we discuss this issue. I come with an open mind and the knowledge that I may have areas where my perspectives need to be expanded or my positions altered. Why take on this sensitive subject? Because I believe that *how we handle issues of inequality in the next several years will prove to be a defining moment in our nation's history.*

For better or for worse.

Why?

Because while all of the corrections and changes we've made thus far to obliterate widespread inequality across all minority groups have been necessary, I believe that we are now *teetering on the edge of overcorrection.* And while at first glance it may seem that an overcorrection in the seemingly "opposite direction" of racism, sexism, prejudice, and oppression could only be a good thing, we must be careful when it comes to rewriting laws, creating policies, and enforcing widespread change.

Because overcorrection has the possibility of creating problems that are just as dangerous as under correction.

It is possible to fix a problem with such force that you end up breaking it in the opposite direction. We have a saying in the military that goes, "If it ain't broke, fix it until it is."

And I fear this has already begun and is continuing to happen.

As we talked about in the second chapter, the road to hell is paved with good intentions and the quest for creating *equal opportunity* for every citizen is beginning to morph into a crusade for creating *equal outcomes*.

This is a subtle yet dangerous shift.

Topics surrounding inequality of any kind—whether that be based upon gender, race, or sexual orientation—are growing more prevalent and heated as time passes. There's a lot of talk right now about "*systemic racism*" and "*systemic oppression*." Racial challenges in our nation have been compared to mass genocide and in response people cry out for drastic action to be taken.

Mass genocide.

That's a pretty large claim. One that's important to talk about.

Because I think there are a lot of people out there asking, "Is there massive systemic racism and oppression going on right under my nose that I didn't know about? Is there a dark underbelly of methodical, rampant brutality and injustice running through the very foundation of our laws and government?"

And if you're relying on the media to give you unbiased facts so that you can logically and accurately assess this issue, you're naive and in for a rude awakening. As we've discussed before, the media thrives on chaos, fear, anger, and offense. When they see a shitstorm they head right for it, stir it up, and see how long they can keep it going. Answers to important questions like whether or not there is rampant, systemic racism or gross inequality taking place in our nation cannot be found by tuning into a news station for a few minutes or scrolling your feed on social media.

This is where our four principles come into play. We'll assess the issue of America's inequalities by applying them so that we can talk about it as clearly and logically as possible.

REMOVE EMOTION

Of all the issues in our nation right now, topics of inequality and injustice are some of the most emotionally charged of any we face. And that's understandable. The whole nature of the conversation revolves around hatred, oppression, unfairness, and prejudice. These have been ugly, toxic elements of our society throughout our history and so it is not surprising that we are faced with strong emotions from all sides as we navigate these topics.

I will not invalidate anyone's right to feel emotion about these subjects. But when it comes to *creating policy and legislation or putting large, systemic measures in place that will affect our society for generations*, it is imperative that we remove emotion from the decision-making process.

Certain chapters of our history will forever contain the stories of oppression, hatred, and injustice that thousands of men and women endured simply because of the color of their skin, their gender, or their sexual orientation. There is immense anger and hurt that has been handed down through generations, created by these past wrongdoings. It's human nature to want justice. And while this ongoing oppression has been put to a stop, the feelings of pain and emotion have continued.

People who feel that they have been wronged want someone to make it right, someone to pay back what was stolen. Everyone desperately wants to find some way to wipe the slate clean and do something to erase the dark lines that run through our history.

This quest to right past wrongs has been the justification behind initiatives such as affirmative action, mandatory diversity hires, policy changes, and the creation of new laws. And it is these very actions that place our nation directly at risk for overcorrection. While these measures seem good, right, and justified, they are the very thing that is shifting our society toward the thinking that all people should be ensured *equal outcome* rather than *equal opportunity*, that bad behavior, hateful comments, or rude attitudes should be legislated and outlawed.

People are crying out for massive, widespread action for a massive, widespread problem. You have women standing up and saying that there are gross disparities between the compensation of men and women. You have people screaming that police brutality and racial oppression is happening *all the time, all around us* and crying out for severe action to be taken such as defunding our police system and changing our laws.

And so the argument goes something like this: "This group of people had the deck stacked in their favor for hundreds of years.

This group of people has had it stacked against them. It's about time we turn the tables and stack the deck in the opposite direction for a change." At first glance, it might seem like an easy way to make things even, fair, and equal.

But while there is a tidal wave of sickening, undeniable proof that our nation allowed the systemic oppression of many minority groups *in the past*, we need to know exactly how much of that we are facing *right now*.

Because while many of us would give anything to heal the wounds and undo the atrocities of the past, *we cannot create laws and policies as an apology for past wrongdoings.*

That's why we need to know what we're facing. So here's the question. *Are there widespread laws, policies, and entities in place that are systemically oppressing our citizens, **right now**?*

We cannot answer this question based upon feelings and emotions. We must answer it by looking *at statistics and analyzing data from a trusted source*. One of the most effective ways to assess a situation without emotion is to look at the numbers.

Let's take a look at the data on racially motivated police brutality.

According to statistics from the FBI through UCR, in 2019, the percentage of Black males being killed by police officers per capita is higher than White males. Though police killed far more White men than Black men, that is simply due to the fact that there are more White males than Black males in the population.

However, out of 328 million people in our country, which has just shy of 700,000 police officers, *the number of cases where police interactions with an unarmed African American suspect resulted in the police shooting and killing the individual was ten.* That's for the entire year of 2019. In five of those cases, the unarmed individual was physically attacking the officer when lethal force was used—a fact which was proven by dashcam evidence. In the other cases where an attack was *not* involved, two of the police officers were charged with murder and two were not. Of the two that were not charged, one involved a female officer who was tackled and another involved an officer whose gun went off unintentionally.

If any of those ten people who were shot were a close friend of mine, I would be absolutely devastated by the loss and feel a whole host of emotions on their behalf. Their lives are important and they matter.

Having said that, I don't believe that there is data or numbers to support the conclusion that right now, in the United States, *there is mass genocide* and *widespread racial oppression on a systemic level.* There is not enough evidence to back these claims. Is there data to prove that there was systemic racial oppression and brutality in years past? You bet your ass there was. And we've worked incredibly hard as a nation to change that.

Are there still horrible people who inflict racially motivated hateful acts on others? Yes. Just as there are still horrible, hateful people who rape children and murder their neighbors. As *individuals,* our hearts can and should empathize with the friends and families of those affected in these situations and incidents. But can we prove that this is *intentionally and systemically* continuing to take place on a wide scale *today*? I have looked, researched, and asked this question repeatedly and as of yet, I have not been able to find any provable data to support this.

The data and numbers on a statistical level do not support the claim that this is a rampant, widespread, systemic problem that requires *extreme measures* such as abolishing our police force, creating new legislation, or making massive policy changes.

And we cannot make large-scale decisions based upon emotions such as anger, offense, guilt, empathy, or regret.

Let's take a look at data on another major inequality issue: the gender pay gap. According to the US Bureau of Statistics, in 1979, which was the first year for which comparable earnings data are available, women's earnings were *62 percent of men*'s. In 2017, women who were full-time wage and salary workers had median usual weekly earnings that were *82 percent of those of male* full-time wage and salary workers. Most of the growth in women's earnings relative to men's occurred in the 1980s and 1990s. Since 2004, the women's-to-men's earnings ratio has remained *in the 80 to 83 percent range.*[20]

At first glance, the approximate 20 percent difference is troublesome. These numbers are the basis for most of the arguments in favor of policy change regarding women in the workplace. But upon taking a closer look, the same study states that, "The earnings comparisons in this report are on a broad level and *do not control for many factors that can be important in explaining earnings differences, such as job skills and responsibilities, work experience, and specialization.*"

---

20 "Highlights of Women's Earnings in 2017," *BLS Reports*, August 1, 2018, https://www.bls.gov/opub/reports/womens-earnings/2017/home.htm.

According to PayScale, a compensation software and data company that pioneered the use of big data and unique matching algorithms to power the world's most advanced compensation platform to help ensure fair wages, women earned $0.81 for every dollar earned by a man. There was a 2 percent improvement from 2019 to 2020 and a 7 percent improvement from 2015 to 2020, when the median salary for men was roughly 26 percent higher than the median salary for women. Even so, the gap still appears rather large.[21]

But in this same study, they go on to state that, "This figure is representative of the uncontrolled—or 'raw'—gender pay gap, which looks at the median salary for all men and women *regardless of job type or worker seniority.*" These are factors you can't simply leave out.

So what is the gender pay gap once all factors such as experience, industry, and job level are accounted for?

The study states, "When men and women *with the same employment characteristics do similar jobs,* **women earn ninety-eight cents for every dollar earned by an equivalent man.**"

Ninety-eight cents for every dollar.

That's what the data shows us. So to say that there is a "massive disparity" between men and women's pay is not an accurate statement. Things like industry and job level, experience, and specialization *must be* accounted for in a study comparing pay.

---

21 "The 2020 Gender Pay Gap Report Reveals that Women Still Earn Less for Equal Work," *PayScale*, March 24, 2020, https://www.payscale.com/compensation-today/2020/03/the-2020-gender-pay-gap-report-reveals-that-women-still-earn-less-for-equal-work.

It's common sense. A 2 percent difference that is proven to be shrinking every year is not mass oppression.

I have had numerous conversations about these subjects with friends of mine who fall into various minority categories and so far no one has been able to help me find the hard numbers or examples that would prove *current systemic oppression on a large scale.*

It is not unkind, unfeeling, or unfair to make this statement. And yet oftentimes when a statement like this is made, it is met with a tidal wave of emotions and a collection of personal stories that go to prove that racism and sexism still exists in our world.

"I could tell you a hundred personal stories about minorities enduring prejudice that would break your heart..."

"You don't know what kind of sexual harassment I endured at my last job."

"You don't know the prejudice my son faces at his school."

And you know what? They would be *exactly right.*

There is still racism and sexism in our world.

There are still oppressors and haters and perpetrators and bigots and humans of the worst kind.

But is there current, widespread, systemic oppression that requires drastic action on the part of law and policy makers? Not from any data that I can see.

This is why *it is vital* that we, as individuals, separate our feelings and emotions tied to hard or unfair situations that we have *personally experienced* before making claims that there is widespread oppression that requires drastic actions like changing laws and policies in our nation.

Are there still racists out there who say and do shitty things? Yes. Are there still sexist pigs in the workplace? Yes. Are there still hateful homophobes out there? Yes. Unfortunately, there are also rapists, murderers, and thieves in our country as well. But just because someone was murdered in your city doesn't mean that there's a widespread uprising of murderers sweeping the nation. It's tragic, awful, and troubling to be sure. The simple fact is that when you have a large collection of people in one location, you're always going to have a percentage of them that are mean, hateful, prejudiced motherfuckers who cause harm and pain to others.

But simply because you have encountered racist, sexist, homophobic people in your life does not prove that we, as a nation, are facing *mass* genocide or *widespread, systemic* racism that requires *drastic, governmental action.*

If my daughter was raped while walking home from school as a teenager, I would be outraged and I would have every right to be. I'd kill the motherfucker if I had the chance. But it would be inappropriate to channel this rage into a campaign to outlaw all males from walking down the street because I came to the conclusion that this is such a widespread, rampant problem that it warrants this kind of severe response.

We cannot allow emotions caused by terrible people to lead us to believe that there is a more widespread problem than there is. We cannot allow hurts, carried through the years from past wrongdoings, to rationalize taking from someone else simply because they resemble the appearance of the past oppressors. If you take any group of people and go far enough into their ethnic lineage, you're going to find a point in time that they got the shit end of the stick. Does that mean that their descendants should have a pass for the rest of eternity? No. They should be provided with equal opportunity to be sure, but that doesn't mean that they should be guaranteed equal outcome because they were wronged at some point in time.

And while there are not any data or studies that I can find to back the claims of current mass, systemic oppression, there are many concrete examples of the contrary. You can find women and people of color represented in all positions across the country and that number grows every day. If the system was still rigged against these minority groups, would that be possible? I don't think so.

When bringing up this fact, I often hear the statement made, "But they had to work twice as hard to achieve the same outcome as a White, straight male in the same position." To this, my question is, "How do you know that?" I know it feels as though this is true, but how is this provable? By what metric can you claim that you had to work twice as hard as someone else? It would be like saying, "Well, it's twice as hard for me to run fast as it is for you." Unless there is some specific, medically documentable reason why, the average person cannot fairly make a claim like that.

How do you know that getting into college was twice as hard for you as it was for me? How do you know that getting the job promotion was more difficult for you than it was for me? Of course there were people in your life who didn't believe in you or said shitty things to you because of your race, gender, or sexual orientation, but can you show any data that proves that *the entire infrastructure of our system* is unfairly biased?

We cannot allow emotions and feelings to inhibit our ability to clearly and logically make decisions. While it's a wonderful thing to be moved with emotion within your personal life to extend acts of kindness or a leg up to your fellow man, laws and policies cannot be created based upon empathy or regret. If my daughter was raped while walking home from school, a law that prohibits all males from walking the streets will only create a whole new set of problems. We must punish illegal and violent acts to the fullest extent of the law, we must oppose attitudes of hatred or oppression in our circles of influence, but there is no data to support the need for severe action in terms of our current laws and policies.

The danger of this sway toward overcorrection is that we are now beginning to see unfair biases in the opposite direction. Large companies are now pressured to make diversity hires and even fill certain quotas for minority hires. *This means that race and gender are once again part of the deciding factor as to who gets a job over expertise, experience, and qualification.*

I can tell you from my own experience as a Navy SEAL instructor that I was pulled aside on more than one occasion and told that there needed to be more Black men on our SEAL teams and that it was up to us, as instructors, to make sure they made it through the program. As a result, I did see bias take place on a number of occasions in Special Forces training, but it was absolutely, 100 percent of the time in favor of the minority and caused by pressure to ensure *equal outcome* rather than equal opportunity.

If you don't want to live in a society in which it is okay to choose people for a job or university or position of power based upon their gender or skin color, then don't put laws in place that focus on gender and skin coloring in the name of equality.

While the strides we made as a nation for equality were necessary and worthwhile in the past, we're crossing into the dangerous territory of overcorrection and emotions have played a huge role in that. That's why it is vital that we remove emotion in order to clearly assess the data on this subject before we draw conclusions or take large-scale action.

REMOVE POLITICS

Inequality issues, like almost all other issues in our country, have become extremely politically charged. And where there are emotionally charged issues, you can bet your ass that you'll find vultures swooping in to use the situation for political gain. This issue in particular has become very politically polarized. Many people assume that the Democratic Party and left-leaning individuals are and *always have been* anti-racist, anti-sexist, and anti-oppression. Many people also assume that the Republican Party and right-leaning individuals fall on the opposite end of the spectrum. Historically, this is simply not the case.

The Ku Klux Klan (KKK), founded in 1865, extended into almost every southern state by 1870. It became a means of opposition, a White southern *resistance to* the **Republican Party's** Reconstruction-era policies which were aimed at creating and establishing political and economic equality for Black Americans.

KKK members waged an underground campaign of violence, coercion, and intimidation which was directed at White and Black Republican leaders. Though Congress passed legislation in an effort to curb Klan terrorism, the reestablishment of white supremacy, *fulfilled through Democratic victories* in state legislatures, remained the organization's primary goal across the South in the 1870s.

This assumption regarding the historical standing of the Democratic and Republican parties has caused many people to blindly believe that they simply need to vote with the left to stay on the "correct side" of racism and sexism. This perception and conclusion are incorrect.

I also believe that the issues surrounding racism and sexism have been used as a powerful weapon in the political arena. The accusation that someone is racist or sexist carries a weight and power in this day and time that is career-ending. Unfortunately, this weapon is used frequently. When faced with political opposition or disagreement, claiming that the other person is racist is the ultimate "checkmate." Like accusations of rape or child molestation, the accuser hardly has to give proof that it happened. The claim is enough to taint the other person forever. You see this strategy used all the time in politics today. Not only does this perpetuate even more political bias and polarization, it also creates chaos and confusion. With accusations like these being thrown around constantly in the political arena, how can the average person hope to assess who to vote for accurately, who to support? And while it may be the ultimate checkmate, it also reduces the credibility of the one making the claims.

Words like "racist," "sexist," and "homophobic" are too often used by politicians and media to create the emotionally charged chaos that has proven so effective in making the minds of the average person pliable, swayable, and easy to manipulate. I believe that is why issues of inequality have gained so much momentum over the past several years. It's perhaps one of the most powerful tools to wield in the game of politics. In our media-driven world, perception is everything. By creating a perception that someone is racist, sexist, or opposed to people of a differing sexual orientation, you can end entire political careers.

If we're going to assess these issues rightly, we must remove all preconceived ideas and biases regarding the topic. Don't assume that one political party is racist and the other isn't. Don't believe every accusation made against political leaders. And don't allow politicians to use this issue to perpetuate their own agendas by tugging at your emotions or feeding you biased or unproven information.

MIND YOUR OWN FUCKING BUSINESS

Topics of inequality all seem to go back to one cornerstone belief: *That someone, somewhere has it easier than you do.* That if things were *actually fair*, your life would be different.

There are places in this world that I have seen with my own eyes where people are oppressed and systematically victimized. It's heartbreaking. It's an existence that no human should ever have. If this kind of brutal, tyrannical power was spreading through our nation today, I'd be the first to lead the charge against it. But again, there is no data to prove this that I can find.

We should all be *very* careful making claims like these. We should also be *very* careful using claims of inequality and unfair treatment as an excuse for our choices and the state of our lives. Claims such as these place blame and focus on others, on their choices and wrongdoings. It holds *someone else* responsible for *our* problems and setbacks. And it serves as a very clever distraction from the one thing that we can actually control—ourselves.

Even if you are a trust-fund baby born into a million-dollar mansion and given every tiny thing your precious fucking heart desires, there will be someone in the world who has it better than you. If you are born into total poverty, abused, and given the short end of the stick at every turn, there will always be someone in the world who has it worse than you.

This quest for "equal outcome for everyone" has caused a whole society to obsessively compare their life against everyone else's—*spending more time trying to make sure that the game is fair than actually playing the game.* There are enough inspiring stories across our planet of people who were born into poverty, abuse, wartime, disease, and any number of horrible, impossible situations that found it within themselves to push beyond their challenges and create a good life, despite the odds. These stories prove over and over again that it can be done.

If we were actually facing mass genocide or widespread, systemic problems, then this would be a different conversation.

We'd be strategizing, we'd be forming a plan to take action at the highest level. But without proof of current, widespread oppression from a governmental level, the responsibility falls to the *individual* to make the necessary choices to create the life that they desire. Falling into the trap of continually identifying as a victim and comparing one's life to another will only deter the achievement of that goal.

So refuse to enter the *"who has it worse"* pissing contest. Don't fall into the trap of constant comparison. Don't blame every challenge you come up against on someone else. Don't spend your life waiting for some law or policy to come along and change everything for you.

If someone tells you that you couldn't be successful because you have a vagina instead of a penis, *fuck them.*

If someone tells you that you couldn't be wildly wealthy and powerful because of the pigment of your skin, *fuck them.*

If someone fires you from a job because you came out as being gay, *fuck them.*

Pick yourself up and do it anyway. Prove them to be the assholes they are. And then revel in the sweet revenge of proving them wrong.

HOLD YOURSELF TO THE SAME OR HIGHER STANDARD AS YOU DO OTHERS

In a conversation about fairness and equality, there is a surprising amount of inconsistency and hypocrisy. Let's look at a few examples where these double standards show up.

Affirmative Action and Diversity Hires

It baffles me that the very measures put into place for the purpose of "obliterating racism and sexism," such as affirmative action and diversity hires, *revolve solely around an individual's race and gender.* There's a startling double standard here.

Think about this for a moment. If there were job positions and university scholarships reserved exclusively for White men, how would people react? They would be appalled. Angered. Outraged. But when job positions and university scholarships are reserved for females or minority groups, it's suddenly called "anti-racist." Shouldn't the entire goal of anti-prejudice measures be to create a world in which individuals are evaluated based upon their character, expertise, and merit rather than gender or skin color?

Among those who cry out for equality the loudest, there is a distinct lack of holding oneself to the very standards being fought for. These double standards will only cause more problems the longer they remain in place. While things like affirmative action or diversity hires may seem like a good short-term fix, designed to "level the playing field," solving an issue of unfair advantages with more unfair advantages isn't going to solve anything.

Take the 2020 presidential race. Joe Biden, who upholds himself up as an anti-racist and anti-sexist model of perfection, went on record saying that his vice-presidential candidate would be a woman and a woman of color. He said this before he even began his search for a running mate. That means if you were White or if you were a man in 2020, you had a 0 percent chance of being Joe Biden's vice president. A public statement such as this sets the precedent that it's okay to allow race and gender to be two of the most important factors in choosing a candidate. People applauded him as a "voice of equality" when nothing about his statements was based on equality, and in fact, it proved bias and inequality in his decision-making process. If he were to have gone on record saying he was only going to consider White men for the job, people would lose their fucking shit. People need to hold themselves to the same standard or higher as they hold others to. And you're never going to solve inequality with more inequality.

Prejudgment and Prejudice

Just as it's wrong for me to come to the table with preconceived notions about someone simply because they have black skin, it is also wrong for someone else to come to the table with pre-conceived notions about me or my beliefs because my skin is white. It's wrong both ways. If you want to uphold equality and get rid of prejudice around skin color, *all assumptions regarding someone's character based upon their skin color* must be removed.

In summary, I would say this. I am all for equality. I'm all for standing up to hateful assholes and oppressors when you encounter them in your life. I'm all for putting a stop to things that steal the freedoms of any citizen in our nation. But while there have been many heartbreaking incidents where racial hate was shown at its worst, we must keep in mind that the numbers indicate that these are just exceptions rather than the norm. This fact should inform how we react and what actions we take and support in terms of laws, policies, and large systemic changes.

I also believe that equality should be equality...across the board. Unfortunately, many of the measures I see being put into place to combat sexism and racism are just another form of rigging the system based upon sex and race. Two wrongs don't make a right. And we would be wise to exercise extreme caution as a nation in how we navigate these issues.

Lastly, I strongly believe that many of the powerful people who cry out the loudest for more affirmative action and more diversity hires and more massive policy changes are actually the ones promoting a form of racism of the worst kind. And here's why.

Have you ever watched an adult play a game with a child and rig it so that the child can win? The adult knows that they are the bigger, better, more qualified player and that there is no way that the child could ever win unless measures were put into place to tip the game in their favor.

To me, that is exactly what many of the initiatives created in the name of equality communicate. It implies, reiterates, and reinforces the notion that straight, White men are the bigger, better, more qualified players. If given an equal shot, people of color, women, and other minority groups don't stand a chance. So the game needs to be rigged. Because only with special treatment will others achieve the same outcome as their White, male counterparts.

Isn't this kind of thinking racism in its ugliest and most sinister form?

Women and people of color are just as capable of achieving success on their own—without the game being rigged. To me, the belief that individuals of color are capable of getting into a university without any special help or that women are just as capable of getting a large promotion based solely upon their own work ethic shows far more respect than the idea that they need special accommodations to make it. Not only is this idea disrespectful and demeaning, it also reinforces the notion that one group of people is stronger and better equipped for life.

Additionally, by rigging the system in one person's favor over another, it robs individuals of the knowledge that they achieved success solely based upon their own merit. When you achieve something in your career or personal life, there's nothing like laying your head on your pillow at night with the satisfaction of knowing that you earned that victory because of your own hard work and choices. To rob anyone of that satisfaction and personal validation is the worst offense of all and to me, the ugliest form of prejudice there is.

In wrapping up, I want to offer a few thoughts I have on actionable things that each one of us can do in our own lives as it pertains to this particular issue.

STOP PASSING DOWN THE PAIN AND BIASES OF THE PAST

As we've discussed, parts of our nation's history are dark and filled with the oppression of both minorities and women. The only way that we can move beyond these wounds is to allow the scab to heal. The more we call attention to the wound and the more we pick at it and show it to others, the more it will continue to bleed.

The statement has been made that racism is not genetic, it's taught. I believe this with all of my heart. No one is born a racist. We are taught behaviors and biases from the people around us. If we want to abolish any remnant of racism, inequality, and the perception that one group of people wields the power while the other is rendered the victim, we must be vigilant about the words that come out of our mouths—especially in front of the next generation.

As harmful as it would be for a White man to sit his son down and tell him that he is privileged and more qualified for achieving success simply based upon his skin color and gender, it's equally as harmful when children of color or young girls are preconditioned to see their race or gender as a disadvantage.

Instead of conditioning children to see their race or gender as a setback and preparing them to be treated unfairly because of it, maybe we should change the conversation. Maybe we should stop focusing on it altogether. Maybe we should start placing a premium on hard work, taking responsibility, and making consistent choices that will set them up for success.

DON'T CREATE OR SUPPORT BIASED POLICIES

I won't beat a dead horse, but fighting bias with more bias just won't work. Policies *must* be impartial and there should be absolutely no wiggle room on that. They should not change, bend, or break based upon a person's race or gender. Whether underhanded or overt, the outcome of biased policy will always be the same. It will only perpetuate the perception that certain individuals are inferior based upon their race or gender—which is the textbook definition of racism and sexism. Unbiased policy is actually the only way to promote true equality.

DON'T MUDDY THE WATERS WITH UNINFORMED SOCIAL MEDIA POSTS

Issues of equality are a hot-button topic and a subject that is frequently posted about on social media. Unfortunately, people are quick to jump on media bandwagons and align with whoever and whatever appears to be on the "correct" side of an issue without much thought or research. This goes back to the sheep/herd mentality that we've talked about before as well as the virtue signaling culture that is so prevalent today. Sharing informational infographics, statistics, and headlines in the name of "educating others" has become common. People share information constantly, usually without investing much time in careful research, fact checking, and corroborating the facts to ensure that the things they are sharing are indeed true. Unfortunately, this is how misinformation is spread and perpetuated. It's how conversations become convoluted and confusing. It's also how organizations and people with ulterior motives and agendas gain traction and power.

Your social media is an extension of you. Whatever you say on social media should be something that you would verbalize publicly in a town hall meeting. You can use the same four principles that we implemented in this chapter as a guide for your social media. Remove emotional and political blinders when talking about an issue, check yourself to make sure you're minding your own fucking business, and hold yourself to the same or higher standard as others.

Both in social media and in conversation, it's important that you and I take responsibility for what comes out of our mouths. Spreading misinformation, spewing our emotions on the public, virtue signaling, blindly buying into a political agenda, and practicing hypocrisy do far more harm than good.

LEAD BY EXAMPLE

This isn't the first time I've said this and it won't be the last. If there is something you want to see changed, *lead by example*. Each of us is given the power to choose what our lives will stand for. If we want to hand our children a better world than we were given, it's up to us to make that happen. If we want to see the next generation soar, we must refuse to hand them the wounds and fractures of the past.

May we form our beliefs with solid, proven truth and steep them in sound logic. May we judge one another solely on character, talent, and capability. And may we each stand for true equality, refusing to settle for any substitute for it.

CHAPTER 9

★

GUNS

S o let's talk about guns. This is another issue that is surrounded by a shitstorm of strong emotions, political agenda, and angry people so accustomed to the noise of their own opinions that they cannot hear anything else. And somewhere in the middle is a large portion of the population asking, "Should people own guns in this century? Should there be more regulations? What about the use of guns in murders, mass shootings, and suicides?"

Questions like these are a great starting point for conversation. Unfortunately, actually *having* any kind of levelheaded conversation about the subject is almost impossible when people can't even discuss guns and gun ownership without releasing a torrent of emotions. Most attempts at real conversation crash before they even leave the runway. You and I are going to set a new precedent here. We'll break this issue down using our four principles as with every other issue we'll discuss. Before we do that, let's take a minute and look at both sides of the argument.

On one hand you have people, like me, who believe that it is the right of any upstanding American citizen to own a firearm. Guns have been a part of our nation's history since the very beginning. They are clearly protected by the first laws ever written in our nation. They also serve numerous purposes—from personal protection to hunting. To me, the greatest advantage that guns provide is the unparalleled ability to *equalize power*. Take a 120-pound, five-foot-four female and by simply giving her a firearm, she has the ability to equalize the power between herself and a murderous, roided up, 220-pound man hopped up on meth. The moment that revolver comes out of her purse, she has equalized the violence disparity, the strength disparity, and the intent disparity between her and her assailant. I don't know of another tool that is more effective in equalizing power.

On the other hand, you have people who believe that guns are to blame for the violence in our nation. That they shouldn't be on the streets. That no good and decent person should own one. That they have no place in the twenty-first century. That guns should be banned from the general public. That we would all be far safer without them.

"How many mass shootings have to happen before we ban guns?"

"You don't need *that* gun to shoot a duck—it should be illegal!"

"How can anyone in their right mind keep a gun in the house with children?"

"If guns were illegal, we would see a decrease in suicides, murders, and mass shootings. Anyone who can't agree with that is as bad as the people pulling triggers."

"What kind of heartless person would rather have the ability to own a gun than protect the safety of innocent children going to school each day by getting them off the streets?"

Statements like these are often made when the topic of guns is broached. They brim with emotion and leave little room for disagreement in their presentation.

Once again, you have an issue with two views on opposite ends of the spectrum. People either run and take sides or get caught in the middle, unsure of what to think. Emotions fly, politics are thrown in, and before long it's hard to tell if the issue is even about guns anymore. Let's pull back the layers and quiet the noise so we can assess this issue clearly and logically.

Let's start by removing emotions.

REMOVE EMOTIONS

Again, the most effective way to assess an issue without emotion is to look at the data. Numbers are unbending. They aren't Republican or Democrat. They aren't empathetic or angry. They don't change based upon what we *feel* is true, what we *want* to be true, or what we *don't want* to be true. They simply tell us what *is* true.

So, let's talk about guns and death. According to the CDC, "In 2018, there were 39,740 firearm-related deaths in the United States—that's about 109 people dying from a firearm-related injury each day. Six out of every ten of those deaths were firearm suicides and more than three out of every ten were firearm homicides."[22]

So, let's break those numbers down a little bit more. According to the Pew Research Center, "In 2017, six-in-ten gun-related deaths in the US were suicides (23,854), while 37 percent were murders (14,542), according to the CDC. The remainder were unintentional (486), involved law enforcement (553) or had undetermined circumstances (338)."[23]

The thing that these numbers show is the undeniable fact *that overwhelmingly, deaths involving firearms were at the hands of individuals with intent to kill or intent to die.* To accomplish this goal, these individuals chose a firearm. The truth is that a firearm is one tool on a table filled with numerous others that could have been used to complete the same task.

Even in a world without guns, demented and evil people will still exist. Depressed and hopeless people will still exist. Violence and murder are as old as human history; it's a dark thread that weaves its way throughout time—far before the invention of firearms. Depression and mental health issues have also been a part of human existence, long before anyone knew what a rifle or handgun was. Study history and you will quickly

---

22 "Firearm Violence Prevention," *Centers for Disease Control and Prevention*, May 22, 2020, https://www.cdc.gov/violenceprevention/firearms/fastfact.html.

23 John Gramlich, "What the Data Says about Gun Deaths in the US," *Pew Research Center*, August 16, 2019, https://www.pewresearch.org/fact-tank/2019/08/16/what-the-data-says-about-gun-deaths-in-the-u-s/.

✳ **GUNS** ✳

see that a human with an intent to kill or to die will always find a way. Many of the bloodiest chapters in human history took place without the use of a single bullet.

Just as a surgeon has a table of tools to help him complete a surgery, there is a whole array of items, substances, and means by which people can choose to end their life or accomplish evil intent against a fellow human being. If you remove guns from the table, this fact will not change. You would simply have one less tool on the table.

Let's say that Ralf hates Bill Smith because Bill slept with his wife and took his life's savings. Ralf wants to murder him and spends his afternoons at the office dreaming up how he will do it. He has numerous ways he can accomplish his evil plan—many of which do not include a gun. A gun may be the most convenient option. But even if Ralf is unable to get his hands on a firearm, his murderous intent for ol' Playboy Bill is not going away. He'll find a way to achieve his goal.

Let's say someone finds themselves in a mental headspace that leads them to make the decision that they no longer want to be alive. Again, there are numerous ways to accomplish this. A gun is one possibility. So is overdosing on medications, hanging yourself, driving your car off the road, and stepping in front of a moving subway. Even if every gun disappeared tomorrow, when someone has crossed over that mental threshold and truly desires to die, they will likely be undeterred by the fact that one tool is missing from the table.

The same is true for mass murder. While a gun may be an easy choice to enact this type of violence, it can still be accomplished without it. There are stories of people driving cars through crowded streets, mowing down dozens of people in a matter of seconds. There are countless stories of bombings, poisonings, drownings, and stabbings throughout history that prove that, when humans thirst for violence, they will find a way.

It's sad. It's disturbing. It's unsettling. Having an emotional reaction toward murder and suicide is completely natural. If one of my daughters were murdered, you better believe a tsunami of emotion would be unleashed. As someone who has had friends who've chosen to take their own lives, I know all too well how heartbreaking it is. But even in the face of these scenarios, my beliefs on the matter would not change. Evil will accomplish what evil wants to accomplish whether or not guns are legal.

Mass shootings are frequently brought up in the gun conversation, especially in the past several years. This particular issue elicits perhaps the greatest emotional response of all subject matters involving guns. And with good reason. There are few things that compare to the level of sickening emotion that immediately springs forth from any normal human at the mention of mass shootings. I don't care who you are, there's no way to watch news reports of a school shooting without your stomach turning.

It's a very natural, human response—one that we should all have. The problem is that these strong emotions often lead people to believe that these incidents are happening *all the time*. This causes people to call for action to be taken, saying, "How many children have to die before we make guns illegal? This is happening constantly. We have to take action; we have to do something about this problem in our nation."

And as much as I would also want to take immediate, extreme action to do *something* in the wake of losing one of my daughters in a school shooting, laws and regulations cannot be created and put into place as a result of strong emotions. They must be the result of carefully analyzed data, based upon fact and logic.

So, let's look at the data. According to the Pew Research Center, "The FBI defines 'active shooter incidents,' 'as one or more individuals actively engaged in killing or attempting to kill people in a populated area.' Using this definition, eighty-five people—excluding the shooters—died in such incidents in 2018.[24]

"The Gun Violence Archive, an online database of gun violence incidents in the US, defines mass shootings as incidents in which four or more people—excluding the shooter—are shot or killed. Using this definition, 373 people died in these incidents in 2018."

Let's compare these numbers to other statistics. According to the CDC, "From 2005–2014, there were an average of 3,536 fatal unintentional drownings per year (non-boating related) in the United States—about ten deaths per day. An additional 332 people died each year from drowning in boating-related incidents. About one in five people who die from drowning are children fourteen and younger. For

---

24 John Gramlich, "What the Data Says about Gun Deaths in the US," *Pew Research Center*, May 30. 2020, https://www.pewresearch.org/fact-tank/2019/08/16/what-the-data-says-about-gun-deaths-in-the-u-s/.

every child who dies from drowning, another five receive emergency department care for nonfatal submersion injuries. More than 50 percent of drowning victims treated in emergency departments require hospitalization or transfer for further care (compared with a hospitalization rate of about 6 percent for all unintentional injuries). These nonfatal drowning injuries can cause severe brain damage that may result in long-term disabilities such as memory problems, learning disabilities, and permanent loss of basic functioning (e.g., permanent vegetative state)."

While I am absolutely not minimizing the horrific nature of a human losing their life to a mass shooting, when emotion is removed from the equation and we logically assess the data, according to the FBI's definition of a mass shooting incident, *eighty-five people die from active shooter incidents.* Compare that to the *3,536 people who die from drowning along with an additional 332 from boating-related accidents.* Even by using the Gun Violence Archive's definition, it's still 373 people compared to 3,536.[25]

So, if the goal is truly to prevent the loss of human life, the numbers would implicate a far greater risk in having a swimming pool than a gun. Furthermore, if you are of the belief that it's *the means* used to kill that is to blame for death, then swimming pools pose a far greater threat than guns. Why aren't

---

25 "Unintentional Drowning: Get the Facts," *Centers for Disease Control and Prevention*, October 7, 2020, https://www.cdc.gov/homeandrecreationalsafety/water-safety/waterinjuries-factsheet.html.

people raising awareness for the danger of swimming pools? Why aren't our news feeds and televisions flooded with reports on drowning accidents? Why isn't there a ticker at the bottom of our television screens counting the number of water-related deaths as they tick upward by the day? Why not begin a movement to eliminate swimming pools altogether? Where is the #parentsagainstswimmingpools movement?

"How many innocent children have to drown before society wakes up and finally eliminates swimming pools from our backyards?"

"How dare you put a swimming pool in your backyard or spend a day on the lake when children are dying every day? You worthless, fucking piece of shit. Is the feeling of cool water on your skin and the pleasure of having a backyard water feature worth this mass loss of life?"

There is a startling disparity in media coverage between the number of drownings and the amount of mass shootings in our country today. After all, there are drastically more drowning deaths than there are mass shooting deaths. The fact is that drownings, while sad, just don't get the same news coverage. They don't elicit the same emotional reaction. They don't create waves of shock and make you sick. We don't want to imagine that the media would really be so heartless as to magnify something as horrendous as a school shooting for the sake of holding people's attention, but it's a fact. As we discussed before, the twenty-four-hour news cycle has become a game of out-scaring, out-shocking, and out-horrifying its competition. This means that rage-inducing, politically charged discussions about guns and stories of them being used for the worst kinds of acts are far more effective at capturing the attention of people than talking about swimming pool safety. Even though the numbers clearly show that one claims more lives than the other.

"But pools and guns just aren't the same thing, Mike," you say. "There's nothing inherently *wrong with* water or swimming pools. Drowning is usually caused by people who don't know how to handle themselves in the water. We just need more training and education on swimming and water-related activities."

And that proves my point exactly.

If you don't believe that all swimming pools should be banished because of how many deaths are caused by drowning, then don't tell me that you believe that all guns should be banished because of gun-related murder and suicide or I'll call you a fucking hypocrite. Large bodies of water are not evil. And neither are guns. Guns are nothing more than a mechanism, a tool. If handled properly and treated with respect, they offer a very effective means to accomplish certain tasks. Large bodies of water also, if handled properly and treated with respect, offer many benefits.

The bottom line is that far too many people are ignorant about guns. They don't know how they work, how to use them properly, or the various types that are out there. Most people lack experience with and exposure to firearms to feel comfortable around them. And humans tend to respond to anything they don't understand with fear. There was a time in history when people with epilepsy were outcasts, even hunted down by others, because no one understood the condition. It was shrouded in mystery, feared, and avoided. People whispered about it—believing that people with epilepsy were witches or possessed with some demonic powers simply because they didn't know what a seizure was. Humans fear and avoid things they don't fully understand or have never had experience with.

It is not heartless or callous to look at this issue objectively. This issue so often gets overrun and convoluted by fear, emotion, and misinformation that it's imperative to look at data and numbers before drawing conclusions.

REMOVE POLITICS

I would venture to say that the primary influencer of people's opinion regarding guns is the position of the political party that they associate with. There are far too many people who give over their minds like a slab of pliable clay for politicians and party leaders to mold on both sides of the aisle. Here's what happens. The leading candidate in your political party is anti-guns. You like him well enough and feel like his ideas generally make sense. Your friends seem to think he's a motherfucking world changer and the next Dalai Lama, so you figure, "Hey, if he's anti-guns, I guess I am too. He seems more qualified than I am to assess the issue, so who am I to disagree?"

If everyone practices this kind of thinking, we're in some real goddamn trouble. To follow someone with blind trust and allow them to inform the entirety of your beliefs is a dangerous thing. That same kind of mentality has driven countless nations into the ground throughout time. We need more people who think for themselves. Who look at trusted data and numbers and weigh all sides of an issue before drawing conclusions. Who corroborate the facts they are being told. Who aren't afraid to like someone *and* disagree with them or dislike someone and agree with them. We desperately need more independent minds.

When people's minds are clouded by strong emotions and biased by media sound bites and party lines, there's no way to effectively or logically discuss the topic. So, take a minute and remove your Democratic or Republican glasses. What do *you* believe about this issue? What facts can *you* find from trusted sources on the subject? How does it change your thinking when you remove emotion and politics from the conversation?

MIND YOUR OWN FUCKING BUSINESS

Another significant contributor to the chaos surrounding this issue is that many of the policy makers, law creators, and people in positions of power making the most significant, high-level decisions regarding guns are also completely unfamiliar and ignorant about firearms in general. How can anyone make large, society-changing decisions without any real knowledge of or experience in the matter at hand? The truth is they can't.

We need leaders who know how to stay in their lane and mind their own fucking business by knowing when it's time to bring in experts in a field that they are unfamiliar with or that is beyond their scope of personal experience. Doing so is not a sign of weakness, but strength. If you're going to make decisions concerning gun laws, why not bring in subject matter experts who actually carry guns for a living? Why not ask police officers, soldiers, border patrol, and FBI agents to come together and collectively be a part of the decision-making process? After all, they are the people who've *actually been in gun fights*. They've had to end another human's life with a firearm under the direction of the job they are performing. They are the most vulnerable to gun violence as they seek to serve and protect at-risk communities through law enforcement. Why are we not bringing them into the conversation, seeing what they have to say?

I believe the greatest reason that guidance from these experts is *not* sought after is because their opinion flies in the face of the goal that many politicians are trying to accomplish. The overwhelming majority of people who carry a gun for their job and are daily faced with situations involving guns in the hands of others come out in favor of the Second Amendment. That should tell us volumes. If the very people who daily interact with armed citizens and noncitizens think it's absolutely necessary to protect the Second Amendment, theirs is an opinion that deserves to be listened to, not scoffed at or disregarded.

Any politician who tosses aside the opinions of these subject matter experts in favor of their own ignorant opinions is arrogant and just plain foolish. It is ridiculous to assume that you know better than the people who've devoted their entire lives to the subject when you know jack-shit about the topic.

No politician would arbitrarily dictate which tools a surgeon can and can't use in an operating room without any understanding of the function and use of those tools. It's a ludicrous thought. And yet, politicians who have never shot a gun in their life and have no knowledge about them or experience with them want to create policies, laws, and regulations concerning fire-arms. This is a classic case in which our politicians need to be told to mind their own fucking business, stick to their line of expertise, and enlist the help of subject matter experts instead of contributing to the chaos and misinformation surrounding this subject.

HOLD YOURSELF TO THE SAME OR HIGHER STANDARD AS YOU DO OTHERS

So, let's say you're reading this and you're thinking, "Mike, I get your point. I've put a lot of thought and research into this myself and I still don't think that guns should be legal." If you've arrived at that belief through independent thought and unbi-ased research, I can respect that we disagree. But here's what I would say: "Lead by example then." If you don't want firearms to be legal, make sure you don't own one, support guns in any way, or allow yourself to benefit from them. There's a startling number of people who supposedly hold "anti-gun" political beliefs and still own a gun. They say, "Well, until it's illegal, I feel better owning one if everyone else is going to."

My response?

Fuck you.

Don't say you agree with and believe in something and then refuse to put it into practice in your own life.

If you're someone who believes in banning guns but wants armed security to make you feel safer at a concert or inside your gated community, you're a hypocrite. And I'll say it again.

Fuck you.

If you think that guns are evil and unnecessary, then you should hold yourself to the same standard as you hold everyone else to. You shouldn't benefit from the protection of firearms if you also believe in getting rid of them.

Case in point: During the presidential election of 2020, Joe Biden stood up and promised bans and regulations on certain guns while a posse of armed Secret Service surrounds him and protects him daily. The irony, the hypocrisy, is undeniable. If you don't believe that citizens should have the right to protect themselves with firearms, then you should model and uphold the same standard in your own life. I can respect someone who is educated and well-informed and who practices exactly what they preach, but I have no tolerance for people who practice hypocrisy and double standards.

Another point I'd like to add here, one I'll reiterate a few times in this book, is that our laws are in place to protect all citizens' freedom and rights. That means that people are going to do things that you don't like and don't agree with. If you are a Bible-thumping Southern Baptist pastor and want the freedom to worship and practice your religion as you see fit, then you should also understand that the exact same freedom should protect another person's right to marry someone of the opposite sex and practice *their* belief system as they see fit.

Guns have been a part of our society since our nation's beginning and are protected by our constitution. Just because you don't agree with them doesn't mean they need to be banned. Laws only matter when people *don't* agree with each other. No one spends time creating laws that protect your right to take a fucking bubble bath because there aren't any anti–bubble bath folks out there (that I know of anyway). To only support "freedom" in the areas you agree with is illogical, hypocritical, and goes against the entire idea of freedom and democracy in the first place.

At this point, I hope the issue is becoming a little less politically and emotionally charged. I hope that your mind is stretching its arms and legs now that it has some breathing room to expand and explore the topic without the pressure of outside influence. Keep asking questions, keep chasing information. Familiarize yourself with all aspects of this subject and listen to people with a variety of perspectives on the matter.

To that end, I'd like to offer a few of my own thoughts and opinions.

APPLY THE MICRO/MACRO TEST

This issue is the perfect time to apply the micro/macro test that we've used previously. In this case, we'll use a street fight as our micro example and our nation going to war as the macro example. On a macro level, if evil threatens to overpower our nation, having weapons and people equipped to use them is what protects us. It is also what equalizes the force between us and the harm and danger coming against us. If we were to give up our weapons, we'd be sitting ducks. We would be left helpless to protect or defend ourselves as a nation. The same could be said on a micro level. Guns can be used as a tool to equalize power and prevent citizens from becoming helpless victims in the face of harm and evil intent.

IT'S THE LAW

Our country was founded on principles and laws specifically designed to prevent a tyrannical government or brutal dictatorship from taking over and oppressing helpless citizens. Our founders were very clear that the circulation and ownership of firearms among upstanding citizens is crucial in ensuring that the government cannot oppress its people.

George Washington put it best when he said,

> A free people ought not only be armed and disciplined. But they should have sufficient arms and ammunition to maintain a status of independence from any who might attempt to abuse them. Which would include their own government.

Open any history book and it is abundantly clear that when citizens relinquish all power and render themselves helpless to resist oppression or tyranny, trouble ensues. When a government is able to disarm its people successfully, it gains the power and ability to oppress and abuse them.

Now, don't misunderstand my words in saying that. I'm not an anti-government militia kind of guy who thinks that left-leaning, anti-gun politicians have some secret plan to form a dictatorship and terrorize everyone. That's not my point. My point is that guns and their ownership by upstanding citizens was one of the measures put into place at a foundational level of our government to *protect* and *ensure* that nothing like that could ever happen.

The Second Amendment is law. It states clearly and irrefutably that citizens are free to own firearms. This means that this issue is not a gray area. We're either free or we're not free. We either uphold our laws or we don't. It's like being HIV positive. You either are or you're not. You can't kind of be positive or mostly be positive. You have it or you don't. These are the laws of our government and until our nation goes through the proper process to repeal that law by majority vote, it will, and should be followed and respected.

THE DOWNSIDES OF BANNING GUNS

When the topic of gun control comes up, it is often stated that if guns were illegal the death rate would decrease drastically. This is simply not true. Take a look at countries like Australia or the UK where gun regulations are extensive. The moment gun ownership was made illegal, a black market was created overnight. It's just like drugs. Though it's a felony to buy heroin in the United States, if you show up to LA tomorrow with $300, you can probably get your hands on some in about twenty minutes.

Guns are no different. By pushing gun circulation into the underbelly of the black market, you only invite corruption and an opportunity for the worst kind of people to rise to a position of power as they pursue the lucrative business of secretly producing and selling them. People will continue to purchase them. People will continue to own them. People will continue to use them.

The only difference is that now *the only* people in possession of them are those willing to break the law in order to have them. It means that guns are *only* in the worst and most dangerous hands. You have now created a society in which honest, upstanding, well-trained citizens *do not* possess guns and those who are of low moral character and high ill intent *do* possess them. What's more, everyone knows it. Criminals now have more confidence, knowing that they possess the upper hand in almost all situations in which they intend to use a firearm for illegal actions.

The citizens who would obey the law and turn over firearms if they become illegal are not the ones you need to worry about having one in the first place. It's the people who *don't have an issue with breaking the law anyway* that you need to worry about.

Additionally, when you ban guns, you are only removing one tool from the table. If someone wishes to enact violence on another person, he will not be stopped by a law that forbids him from purchasing a firearm. He will either come by a gun illegally or he will resort to other means. He will use his car, a knife, or a fucking chainsaw.

If there is a disturbed lunatic with an intent to enact violence on a school and no access to a gun, he (or she—I suppose we should give equal opportunity for women to be mass murderers also) could kick down the door of a fourth-grade classroom with a twenty-four-inch blade, STIHL chainsaw, and a full tank of gas and do an incredible amount of damage. In a country where guns are illegal, this would be done without any fear of a citizen having any means to fight back. There would be very little that anyone could do to stop this horrific act. On the other hand, a firearm in the hands of a well-trained citizen would be the perfect power equalizer to immediately stop this type of violence.

Banning guns will only create a dangerous black market and, in some cases, increase death rates by forcing violent and evil people to seek more creative means to carry out their plans to harm.

An antelope will not be safer with its horns cut off.

REGULATIONS AND RESTRICTIONS

When it comes to regulations and restrictions, I believe that the existing regulations in place for purchasing and owning a gun are more than sufficient. Owning a gun is our right and freedom as citizens of the United States of America, and until that changes, there should not be regulations and restrictions that infringe upon it.

I can speak to these regulations from my personal experience. I own a couple dozen guns. I'm not a gun fanatic or the guy with five safes full of guns in a basement somewhere, but I do own a variety of firearms. I've got a couple of rifles, several handguns, and ammunition. It's not a fucking militia cache by any means, but it's a respectable collection. I also have a license to carry in Texas, which is good in thirty-plus other states. I've done all the necessary requirements and background checks to obtain this.

Having said that, if I walk into Bass Pro tomorrow to purchase a firearm, I will still have to go through a background check through the FBI in order to complete the purchase. To me, these measures are completely sufficient. If you pass the FBI background check, which checks for felonies, domestic disputes, arrests, etc., you should be able to purchase and own a firearm. Anything beyond the measures already in place and you are beginning to infringe on people's rights and freedoms.

If there is someone at risk of being a danger to themselves and others to the point that they shouldn't own a firearm, they probably shouldn't be walking the streets. "But shouldn't we talk about mental health?" you'll hear people ask. Okay. You want to talk about mental health? Talk about mental health! But that doesn't have shit to do with guns. If someone is in a mental state that is so messed up that they would be considered a danger to others or themselves if they possessed a gun, then they probably shouldn't be driving down the highway in a vehicle that could be driven into oncoming traffic, in a room with steak knives, or walking our neighborhood streets unsupervised.

If someone has gone that crazy, they will eventually reach for whatever tool on the table is available to them. If someone wants to be violent, they can do it with a chainsaw or a paring knife. If someone wants to harm themselves, they can find a tall building or a piece of rope. Are we going to start slapping regulations on gardening tools and ropes? Are we going to start doing a full mental health workup for every person who wants to buy a vehicle or have a meal in a tall rooftop restaurant?

If we go down that path, we are no longer a free country. Freedom means that individuals have the right to choose. If they make a poor choice, they suffer negative consequences for their actions. Regulating every aspect of life will do far more harm than good. Not to resort to a cliché, but increasing regulations on citizens is a slippery slope, one that our nation would be wise not to travel down.

GUNS AND HUNTING

While we are on the subject of regulations, I'd like to give a few thoughts on the subject of hunting since it is often talked about along with gun issues. Hunting is not a personal hobby or interest of mine, but I support citizens' rights to hunt. While I don't think that it's something that should be heavily regulated, I think it's necessary to have some regulations to protect the health of wildlife populations. Many agencies already do this, from fish and wildlife services to local and federal game warden programs. Most regulations revolve around how hunting is conducted and how often it's done.

I think these types of regulations should be determined solely on data gathered about a specific area and the game population in it. They provide needed checks and balances to protect the ongoing health of wildlife by setting limits on the numbers of kills and times of year when hunting is permitted. Having said that, I don't advocate heavy regulations, particularly when it comes to the details of how someone goes about making a kill. If the law says that people are allowed to hunt, they need to be allowed to hunt. If you're allowed to kill five deer, it isn't the job of the government to decide how you go about doing that. Having said that, I would urge you to take a look at your own hunting practices and see if they pass the shopping cart test. And if you aren't familiar with the shopping cart test, I'll explain.

When you finish unloading your shopping cart at the grocery store and shut your car door, you are left with an empty shopping cart, right? You know that there is a specific place for empty shopping carts to go and that putting it there is the right thing to do. Is it against the law *not* to put your shopping cart away? No. Can you get fined for *not* putting your shopping cart away? No. Is there a shopping cart police force? No. But if you push your cart in a vacant parking spot or wedge it between two parked cars because you don't want to walk your sorry ass over and put it in the goddamn cart holder, that makes you an asshole. And if you can't pass the shopping cart test, you're a jerk—a jerk who lacks solid character and basic common courtesy.

The same could be said for certain hunting practices. There are ways to go about killing an animal that are strategic and respectful. And there are ways to go about it that just make you a fucking asshole. It's not the job of the government to legislate good behavior, instill solid morals, teach manners, or make people use common sense unless it's hurting or damaging other people. But if you are knowingly practicing poor and characterless hunting techniques, you're just a shitty person. It doesn't mean that the government needs to babysit your ass in every situation or send you to jail for it. But it does mean that the rest of us are hoping that karma will be the bitch everyone says she is and give you a dose of your own medicine.

As always, I'll close this chapter with actionable things that you can do to be a positive force and lead by example with regards to this issue. Here are a few things that anyone can do when it comes to guns:

EDUCATE AND TEACH CHILDREN HOW TO RELATE TO FIREARMS

Children and young adults need to be taught how to relate properly to firearms. I often hear parents say, "Well, I would own a gun, but I have children in the house." My next question is this: "Do you have a butcher block with knives on your kitchen counter?" The answer is usually yes. "And how did you keep your child from stabbing themselves?" I'll ask.

Upon further questioning, most parents say that they simply taught their children that knives are sharp and dangerous and not to be played with under any circumstances when their children were small. And when the child grew into adulthood they were taught how to properly and safely handle them. This is healthy. As an adult, that child isn't going to panic or lose their shit the first time they see or touch a knife. Because they were taught a healthy respect for the tool and then guided in the proper handling of it.

The same practice should be transferred in relation to guns. Children should be taught to respect the power of the tool and then how to handle it properly when they are of age. This dispels fear and ignorance, which often leads to misuse. In the early 1950s, high schools provided rifle safety and hunting classes for young adults. I think we'd do well to return to this kind of practice. By removing both ignorance and the novelty and mystery that often surrounds guns, I believe that we would have a far more level-headed society in relation to them. Video games and movies shouldn't be the only time that children are exposed to guns. As parents, and as a society, we need to put measures in place to educate our children and prepare our young adults in this area.

Additionally, I would add that as more attention is called to the safety of women in regard to being sexually abused, educating young women in the use of guns as means of self-protection would be a swift and effective way to put a stop to the prevalence of rape and sexual assault. When you have a society in which women are trained and equipped with a tool that equalizes the size disparity between men and women, you better believe the fucking assholes who get off on abusing women are going to think twice about trying to overpower them.

REPLACE FEAR WITH RESPECT

Humans tend to fear what they do not understand. There is so much mystery, fear, and ignorance that surrounds guns and firearms. This is unnecessary. If you were to take someone from the Middle Ages and put them in the driver's seat of a car, they'd probably feel immense fear at the sights, sounds, and capabilities of a moving vehicle. Because they've never been exposed to it, they don't know how to use it, and they have no understanding of it. Whether or not you choose to keep a gun in your house or get a license to carry, you can do your part as an individual to replace fear and ignorance about guns with respect and education.

EDUCATE YOURSELF

The greatest thing you can do in regard to gun issues is to properly educate yourself on the topic before you come to conclusions about it. There are far too many people screaming opinions about the subject who have absolutely no fucking idea what they are talking about, people who've never handled a firearm and who don't know the first thing about them. In my opinion, that would be the equivalent of me going on social media and arguing about the best kind of PMS medication without having any experience and doing absolutely no research on it. *How the fuck would I know?* The truth is, I don't.

Take time to do your own research. Read material from trusted, reputable sources. Don't just repeat the party line or retweet what your favorite celebrity says about it. Your thoughts and conclusions should be yours and yours alone. Your mind is the one thing that you have complete control over. So don't be hasty to side with any position and don't make your mind up quickly. Take time to educate yourself and be a voice of reason. God knows we need more voices like that in our world today.

CHAPTER 10

HUMAN TRAFFICKING

s Americans, we pride ourselves on being the land of the free. Our history books tell the story of how slavery ended and we shake our heads, wondering how anyone in their right mind could have allowed this atrocity to continue for as long as it did. But in our nation today, as we speak, there is a staggering number of innocent people who live enslaved every single day—thousands who are anything but free. And this subject deserves our undivided attention.

Human trafficking is quickly becoming one of the world's largest illicit industries. According to the US Department of Homeland Security, in 2016, an estimated 40.3 million people are in modern slavery, including 24.9 million in forced labor and 15.4 million in forced marriage.[26] Which means there are 5.4

---

26 "Force Labour, Modern Slavery and Human Trafficking," Internal...

victims of modern slavery for every 1,000 people in the world. Sadly, one in four victims of modern slavery is a child. Out of the 24.9 million people trapped in forced labor, 16 million people are exploited in the private sector such as domestic work, construction, or agriculture; 4.8 million people in forced sexual exploitation; and 4 million people in forced labor imposed by state authorities. Women and girls are disproportionately affected by forced labor, accounting for 99 percent of victims in the commercial sex industry, and 58 percent in other sectors.[27]

The money that is generated worldwide from this industry is staggering. Many experts estimate that it tops $150 billion a year. The magnitude of this global problem cannot be overstated and should disturb anyone with a basic sense of human decency. While issues like drug trafficking have been spotlighted for many years, conversations about human trafficking have only begun to see the light of day. It's an industry that has grown and thrived in the dark for far too long. And that has to change.

Across the globe, human trafficking encompasses both the sex trade and forced labor trade. In the United States, the sex trade is most prominent. On our streets, in our shopping malls and parks, and within the walls of our hotel chains and fast-food restaurants lurk masterminds of this trade with the intent to prey upon the innocent. The most common age for sex trafficking victims in the United States is between twelve and fourteen

---

...Labour Organization, September 2017, https://www.ilo.org/global/topics/forced-labour/lang--en/index.htm.

27 Ibid.

years of age, primarily girls. Sickeningly, this is only the average, which means that there are many cases in which children are sold and used for sex as young as three and four years old. These horrendous acts are not isolated events involving a small handful of demented individuals. It is widespread—a growing business of industrialized rape.[28]

And while it may be hard for some to imagine that something so abhorrent could be happening beneath the noses of the everyday American, there's no denying the numbers as studies and statistics emerge on this issue.

In the past, the US Department of State has estimated that 14,500 to 17,500 victims are trafficked *into* the United States each year. This figure does not include victims who are trafficked *within the country* each year. In 2020, Polaris, which holds one of the largest data sets on human trafficking in North America, estimated that there were 22,326 trafficked victims and survivors and identified 11,500 situations of human trafficking. They also identified 4,384 traffickers and 1,912 suspicious businesses. They also saw a 19 percent increase from 2018–2019 of individuals contacting the trafficking hotline. Research also shows that this takes place in every single state across the US.[29]

It's hard to comprehend these numbers. As I look at them, I am outraged and incredulous. As a father of two daughters,

---

28 "Human Trafficking," *US Customs and Border Protection*, January 9, 2020, https://www.cbp.gov/border-security/human-trafficking.
29 "2019 US National Human Trafficking Hotline Statistics," *Polaris*, November 12, 2020, https://polarisproject.org/2019-us-national-human-trafficking-hotline-statistics/.

I am outraged that innocent children just like them are being raped and abused daily. I am incredulous as someone who has dedicated their life to fighting for freedom, that this could be happening on American soil—right under our noses, without us doing more to stop it.

A good friend of mine, Jeremy Mahugh, a former Navy SEAL sniper, co-founded Deliver Fund, a nonprofit intelligence organization dedicated to combatting human trafficking. Their team utilizes decades of experience from the team's careers in the CIA, NSA, Special Operations, and law enforcement. They leverage cutting-edge technology into the ultimate weapon against human trafficking. Some of my *Mike Drop* listeners may remember an interview I did with Jeremy about the topic of human trafficking.

Deliver Fund broke down the numbers of the problem we're facing in a way that causes the reality of it to sink in. According to Deliver Fund:

Every two and a half hours, a child is taken by human traffickers.

Roughly 100,000–150,000 victims are held as commercial sex slaves.

Fifty percent of sex-trafficked victims are children.

Ninety-six percent are female.

Every trafficked child is sold an average of 5.4 times per day.

And saddest of all? *The average lifespan of victims once taken is seven years.*[30]

---

30 "Human Trafficking Awareness," *DeliverFund.org*, Sept. 21, 2020, https://deliverfund.org/the-human-trafficking-problem-in-america/.

The stories that come from these victims are unthinkable. Stories of children being abducted or coerced and then held in dog kennels, raped dozens of times per day, force-fed drugs, and violently abused. Stories of children as young as three and four being sold to those who would force unthinkable sexual acts upon them. Stories of being sold twenty times per day, six to seven days a week, for years on end. Is it any wonder that the lifespan of these victims is so low? Who could survive a life like that?

It's clear that something must be done. If there's an issue that deserves awareness and action, it's this one. There are complexities to this industry that will require a strategic course of action to rid our nation of it for good. Again, we'll use our four principles as a framework to help us break it down and assess it from all angles.

REMOVE EMOTION

Anyone with a beating heart (except for the sick fucks perpetuating this scourge on society, obviously) can't read the last few paragraphs and not be filled with some kind of human emotion right now. Anger, compassion, rage, heartbreak. It's all a natural response to the images of innocent children being abused in such hideous ways. Most of us are about ready to cut the dicks off of every one of these abusers and find a nice home for a couple of bullets in the chests of these monsters. But if we're actually going to create effective solutions, we need to remove our emotions and think about this logically so we can form effective and strategic solutions for obliterating this evil for good. Before we do that, I want you to take a step back and ask yourself this question:

Is this a problem that you think needs to be fixed?

I'm going to go out on a limb here and guess that you responded with a yes to that question without a second thought.

Let me ask you another question.

Do you want this to end?

Again, I'm guessing you said yes.

But I'm going to ask you to take a minute, take a deep breath, and really think about what I'm asking you and I'm going to ask it again.

*Do you **really** want this to end?*

I'll assume you said yes again and are wondering why in the world I felt the need to ask it twice. *Isn't this a no-brainer? Who in their right mind wouldn't want to end this kind of evil in the world?*

I have one final question.

Are you willing to do whatever is necessary to fix this problem?

There is a reason I asked you and asked you again. If you said yes to all of these questions, then you need to be prepared to do what it takes to follow through. There *are* solutions for putting an end to this. There are solutions that could be implemented tomorrow that would cut the legs off of this monster. But I'm not going to lie to you, these solutions will require us to take severe action. They will require that bad things be done to bad people.

As a former Navy SEAL who's executed many dangerous operations, I have had a handful of times in my life when I have been forced to look in the mirror and ask myself if I'm willing to take the actions necessary, no matter how ugly, to fight for freedom and oppose evil. The American people are going to need to have the same conversation with themselves before we jump into strategizing on how we fight this atrocity in our nation.

Because one thing is obvious to me. Whatever we are doing right now isn't working. Taking a sympathetic, weak approach toward offenders isn't working. Offering new vocational, rehab, and GED programs to them and thinking that it's going to fix the problem isn't working. The problem is only getting worse and the industry is exploding with new growth every single year. We need to collectively remove our emotions from this situation and get ready to take an extreme approach to an extreme problem. We need to ready ourselves to stomach what it's going to take to annihilate this evil. Because there are no pretty solutions to a problem as grotesque as this one.

So I ask you again, *do you **really** want this to end?*

Okay then. We'll start by breaking down the problem in a logical way and then we'll talk about what it's going to take to end this for good.

There are three key roles involved in keeping this industry alive. Without any one of them, the trade would crumble. They are:

- *The Seller (a.k.a. trafficker):* the one who provides the supply. Because the product provided is an actual human being, providing the "supply" involves abduction or coercion. There are many different methods in which this is done. Deliver Fund outlines how this process oftentimes takes place:

o *Targeting a Victim:* Human traffickers use any tools available to them to make a connection to potential victims, such as social media, video gaming consoles, and chat rooms.

o *Scouting Victims/Ideal Characteristics:* The traffickers often search for specific characteristics that make a victim the most vulnerable. This includes emotional neediness, low self-confidence, and economic stress.

o *Manipulation/Gaining Trust:* While looking for the role they can play in a victim's life, traffickers work to obtain trust from the victim through casual conversations over weeks and sometimes over months. Traffickers also send their current victims to interact with potential victims in order to gain trust. These girls essentially act as scouts for the trafficker.

o *Creating Dependency/Filling a Need:* The traffickers utilize the information they gathered to fill a role in the victim's life. Through gifts, love, friendship, drugs, or alcohol, traffickers force the victims into a dependent relationship.

o *Trapping The Victim/Forced Isolation:* With their new role in the victim's life, traffickers wedge themselves between the victim and those closest to them—their friends and family.

o *Abusive Behavior/Maintaining Control:* The traffickers claim a service they offered must be repaid (providing drugs, alcohol, car rides, or cell phones, for instance). They typically demand sex as payment. Then, through threats, violence, fear, or blackmail, the traffickers maintain full control over the victim.

Various traffickers have different approaches. There is the "Romeo" tactic in which the trafficker promises love, affection, relationship, gifts, money, etc. to the victim as a way of luring them in and eventually taking control and abusing that power. There is also the "Gorilla" tactic in which the trafficker uses force and fear to gain control. This may involve physical abuse, threats to harm a family member or even the victim's child in some cases, threats to deport the victim, and executing extreme violent acts on the victim when orders are disobeyed. This tactic oppresses the victims into submission. Oftentimes, victims are forced into addiction to drugs such as heroin to create a dependency on the trafficker.

Experts agree that for the majority of these traffickers, it's all about the money. The majority of the time, these trafficking rings have nothing to do with any kind of fucked-up religion or ideology. Though anyone willing to go to these lengths for money is more than a little twisted in the head, it's a business fueled by greed and a lust for money and power for most sellers.

- *The Purchaser (sometimes referred to as "The John")*: These are the sick fucks willing to pay money to abuse another human being. Among these are sex offenders, abusers, and pedophiles. These are the ones who have created the demand. Based on how large this problem has grown, it's obvious that there is a hell of a lot more of these sick motherfuckers out there than we would like to think. *And there would be no industry without demand.*

If no one was purchasing these despicable "services," the traffickers would not have a profitable business. There would be no reason to continue abducting and manipulating innocent people into oppression. *We must face the uncomfortable truth that these staggering statistics are created by a whole portion of our population thirsting for this kind of evil and keeping this industry alive.*

- *The Victim (or the person being trafficked):* The one who is being manipulated, oppressed, enslaved, and abused. The psychological trauma and damage done to these individuals is extensive. Some seek freedom and know that they need to find a way out. Some have been ground into submission with such force that they don't even attempt to fight anymore. Some have been so brainwashed that they lose touch with reality and don't even realize that they are being victimized. As statistics show, few can even live for more than a handful of years in that kind of situation.[31]

There are numerous approaches and theories as to the best way to begin to tackle this problem. Some would say that

---

31 "2019 U.S. National Human Trafficking Hotline Statistics." *Polaris*, Nov. 12, 2020, https://polarisproject.org/2019-us-national-human-trafficking-hotline-statistics/.

attacking the supplier is the best route. Some say that demand should be eliminated first. Others try and offer proactive measures to keep victims from being victimized and provide safe spaces in hopes that victims can find a way out of oppression and rebuild their life.

Due to the extent of the problem, it is beneficial to hit it from all angles. We should be doing everything we can to empower law enforcement with as many tools as possible to catch the sellers and we should provide safe places for victims to go. But in my opinion, the only way to eradicate the problem is to eradicate demand. As long as there is a high demand for this industry and people willing to pay for it without the fear of suffering much personal consequence, traffickers will simply get creative and find ways around the law to keep their business thriving. This business is very similar to the drug industry in that regard. As long as there is demand, suppliers will continue to think outside the box and find ways to supply it. Even if trafficking victims are rescued and placed in safe homes, the sad truth is that they will be replaced within a matter of hours with another innocent victim and the cycle will continue. It's all a cat-and-mouse game unless you eliminate the demand. I'm a huge advocate and supporter for efforts that center around the victim and the trafficker, but I believe that first and foremost, we need to work aggressively to eliminate the demand for this entire industry. As soon as the demand is gone, the money is gone, which means that the industry crumbles.

How would I propose eliminating the demand? This leads back to my questions earlier as to how serious you are about eliminating the problem. Because my answer isn't for the faint of heart. There's a reason we're talking about this under the heading of removing emotion.

Create and Enforce Severe Punishment for Offenders

In my opinion, the single greatest way to eliminate demand would be to create and enforce a punishment so severe that it strikes fear into the hearts and minds of even the most hardened criminals. When someone is a criminal, we as a society should see it as our duty to deprive them of their most basic human right—freedom—by placing them in prison. Depending on the crime, there may be varying degrees of provisions given to prisoners, but certain criminals, especially those who have done unspeakable things to the most innocent and defenseless members of our society, *should be placed in conditions that are extreme and harsh.*

We need to create prisons that are designed with the sole purpose of discouraging heinous crimes at the highest level by orchestrating all aspects of the prisoner's experience to be harsh and uncomfortable. Prisoners in these facilities should not be given televisions, gyms, books, beds, blankets, or any access to sunlight and fresh air outside. They should not be given access to YouTube, HBO, telephones to call home, and supplements from the commissary kitchen.

Instead, they should be placed in conditions so severe, so relentless, so awful that should they ever get the chance to leave, they would do so while saying, "I *never* want to come back here again. And I will do whatever the fuck it takes to make sure that I never have to." That should be the mentality of every single criminal who walks out of a prison. If it's not, we're clearly missing the entire purpose of prison in the first place. And it's fairly obvious at this point that we have failed in this regard.

What would this look like? For starters, prisoners would be stripped naked. They would be held in a cell with a toilet and just enough room to sit, stand, and lay. No furniture, no bed, no blankets, no television. In addition to this, prison cells would utilize one of the most effective tools in causing deep discomfort without harming an individual: *they would be cold.* The temperature in these prison cells should be cold enough to make prisoners deeply uncomfortable without causing long-term bodily damage. This lack of basic warmth wouldn't hurt them, it wouldn't harm them in any way. But it would make their prison experience *fucking miserable.* With no bed, no clothing, and no blankets, there would be no escape from the deep discomfort. A naked body against concrete. Rationed food and water, enough to keep you alive. That's it.

Some people may argue that this treatment is inhumane or torturous. But honestly, I don't give a fuck. Being stripped down naked and living in deep discomfort is far less torturous than the things they have done to others. Making living conditions relentlessly cold creates a sense of misery without touching the prisoner, harming the prisoner, or even looking at the prisoner. This one environmental change has the power to make a person absolutely miserable. We're not talking about a jail cell for shoplifters here. We're talking about the worst of society.

Changing the temperature of a prison may sound simple, but as someone who's spent more than my fair share of time subjecting myself to the bitter cold during my training and serving as a Navy SEAL, I can tell you that being cold for a prolonged period of time has a profound effect on the mind. As a SEAL instructor, I have also been given a front-row seat to watch how numerous other individuals have reacted to it. I've watched tough men who've spent their entire lives aiming and preparing to become a SEAL make the decision to throw it all away in one moment simply because they couldn't handle the cold. They were willing to say goodbye to their life's dream and trade it for a little warmth. I've seen six-foot-tall beasts of men cry and whimper like children at the thought of having to get back into the cold water. It's a powerful, powerful tool.

So trust me when I say, if someone is forced to lay naked on concrete and freeze their dick off night after night, with no relief, they will do just about anything to make sure they are never subjected to it again. And let me be clear, when I say freezing your dick off, I do mean this metaphorically. Though personally I wouldn't mind some dicks being permanently damaged by the cold, I'm not proposing conditions quite that harsh, only enough to create deep discomfort. If the prisoner complains and claims that hypothermia is coming on, an anal thermometer can be used to determine their core temperature. I've utilized this method in SEAL training. When recruits would complain and cry hypothermia, I'd send them to the van and let them get their temperature taken with an anal thermometer and trust me, guys were a lot less inclined to complain when they knew that's what would be in store.

With conditions like these in place, sentencing time could also be reduced because the process of mentally breaking down the individual, and teaching them a lesson that won't be soon forgotten, would be accomplished on a much faster timeline. These individuals aren't going to emerge from that kind of facility with their chest out, bragging about how tough they are or writing rap songs about doing time. Word will get out quickly that prison is horrible, miserable, and should be avoided at all cost. This reminds me of using canines in law enforcement. I've watched videocam footage of criminals who are acting big and brave, even while being encircled by police officers, suddenly lay down on the ground in total surrender the moment they see a dog come onto the scene because they have heard stories of the pain that dogs are capable of inflicting.

Does this sound too harsh? Are you thinking, "Oh, but Mike, we couldn't do *that*. That's just cruel."

Because this is where we come full circle and arrive right back at my original question.

Do you want this problem to end? And are you willing to do what it takes?

There's a reason I questioned just how much you actually want this to end. The only way we are going to see a change is if we enforce a punishment so drastic, so awful, that people will avoid it at all cost. Even individuals with the type of desires and impulses that keep the sex trafficking industry alive will think twice about acting on them if they know how severe the consequences of doing so are. Humans are wired for self-preservation and the instinct to keep oneself from that kind of misery will trump the desire to do evil deeds the majority of the time. Don't say you want this problem to end and then shy away in discomfort the moment we get real about what it's going to take. It's obvious that whatever we are doing now isn't working. Sometimes obliterating evil requires us to do things that are uncomfortable. But we cannot afford to sit back and not take swift and forceful action because of our delicate sensibilities while children are being raped and held in kennels and subjected to agonizing abuses every single day.

Study the Lives, Minds, and Genetics of the Offenders

As I stated before, the extent of this problem speaks to the fact that there is a significant portion of the population with an affinity for rape, pedophilia, and all shades of twisted nonconsensual sexual experiences. This should truly alarm us. While we can lay the blame for these evils at the feet of the traffickers, their motivations are a little more straightforward than that of the purchaser. Traffickers are people with greed and a seared conscience. But the purchasers who have created this demand are motivated by something else entirely. It's hard for me to grasp or even begin to wrap my mind around the nature of this problem. I have a hard time understanding what could possibly lead a person to be willing to find, pay for, and enjoy the ability to rape a small child. Many have classified these demented people as animals, but honestly I don't know any animal that is that fucked-up. We need to study this problem. We need to figure out what is causing a portion of our population to hunger and thirst for this.

In my opinion, if we apprehend a pedophile that has raped and abused children, we should be allowed to study them. If they

so willingly treated children inhumanely, to me, they have nullified their right *not* to become a lab rat. I'm not talking about
torture or picking them apart, but I am suggesting that we use
the offenders that we have in custody to help us understand what
factors are in play that create this problem. We need to study
their psychology, their nutrition, their past experiences, and
more. I am a man of science and I believe that there has to be
some common denominators that contribute to the formation of
a human being that craves and acts upon these kinds of impulses.

I am no psychologist, but I have read enough research that
overwhelmingly points out that those who sexually abuse
others were sexually abused themselves,[32] usually as children.
There are also studies that suggest that there could be genetic
factors that contribute to pedophilic disorders. If we can better
understand the factor in play that creates this problem, we can
also better understand how to begin to deal with it.

Again, that's why I believe that apprehended offenders
should be used for these studies—whether they like it or not.
Understanding this problem could help us figure out proactive
methods to reduce the prevalence of these types of behaviors.
On this point I want to make it clear that though I think gaining insight into the mind of offenders would be beneficial, I by
no means think that this should be used as an excuse for their
behaviors and deeds. Even if we identify certain contributing

---

32 Karine Baril, "Sexual Abuse in the Childhood of Perpetrators," Institut
    National de Santé Publique Québec, November, 2012, https://www.inspq.
    qc.ca/en/sexual-assault/fact-sheets/sexual-abuse-childhood-perpetrators.

factors, such as the offender having been victimized, that *does not* excuse their actions and should not cause us to take a sympathetic, weak approach. I don't care what your story is or how horribly you've been treated in the past, if you act upon your impulses to use and abuse an innocent, helpless human being, you should be punished and punished severely. That's the only way that this cycle will end.

Educate Offenders on the Impact of Their Actions on the Victim
The last part of this solution for decreasing demand would be to find ways to educate offenders on the detrimental effects that those types of actions have on victims. This could also be helpful for individuals who are not yet offenders, battling the temptation to act upon sexually abusive impulses. It would stand to reason, given the fact that many of these offenders were victimized at some point in their lives, appealing to their humanity and showing them the detrimental effects these types of actions have on the victim could cause them to think twice about acting upon their impulses.

While I'm sure there are some people out there so twisted in the head that they would actually relish seeing the harm of innocent people, in many cases it would cause the abuser to face the humanity of their victim. Abusers and offenders often find a way to detach and dehumanize the victim so that the reality of what they are doing to an innocent human doesn't fully meet up.

Many people, even successful men (and women in some cases) of power, find a way to rationalize paying for sex with minors. I think many purchasers of these services have so objectified the victim that they block out even thinking about them as a person anymore. The more we educate and show the tragic effects that this industry has on victims, the more we can force offenders (or those toying with the idea) to face reality and come to grips with the kind of pain and anguish their actions cause in other human beings.

By removing emotions, we can look at this problem systematically and strategically. We can also look ourselves in the mirror and see if we've got what it takes to make the tough choices necessary to fight for the innocent.

REMOVE POLITICS

When it comes to human trafficking, it's one of the few issues that I think most people in our country can come together on. This is a human issue that surpasses party lines for most of your average American citizens. However, there are still ways in which political bias has a profound effect on this issue. Anyone who has done much research into the sex trafficking industry will quickly uncover the fact that many powerful people are involved in this industry. Both on the side of the seller/provider and the purchaser, this includes powerful political figures in our country. These people not only continue to keep this horrible industry alive by participating in it, but they also have the means to protect it from those of us who are dedicated to helping expose and put an end to it. And that's something that should deeply disturb the American people.

The sad truth is that far too many people are willing to turn a blind eye toward scandals and reports of suspicious behaviors when it comes to the candidate that they support. The power that political bias has on people never ceases to amaze me. So many people are so blinded by it that they are willing to vote for someone who has been implicated in numerous scandals involving sexual offenses simply because that's who their team chose as the frontrunner. "Oh that's just the media making up stuff because they don't like him," people say. But rarely do they stop and actually research and evaluate if the one on the podium for their political party is *a fucking criminal.*

It's a classic example of the sheep/herd mentality. People are too willing to dumbly follow the pack and assume that everyone else is doing their homework and making sure that the team pick is a good one. Too often people cast their vote because they just assume to follow their political flock, or because they deem one candidate to be the lesser of two evils, or because they know that there are a couple of upcoming Supreme Court appointments and they think that a certain candidate will choose judges that they like. None of these are reasons to cast a vote for someone. This kind of mentality leads a society to be so blind that they can't even see that they are voting for corrupt, greedy pedophiles and sex offenders. This political bias is on *both sides* of the aisle—it isn't relegated to the left or the right. Both sides are guilty of it.

If we are going to see real change, we're going to have to be vigilant to do our research and remove our biases before casting our votes to ensure that our elected officials are upstanding people—not those who would protect an industry as horrendous as sex trafficking.

MIND YOUR OWN FUCKING BUSINESS

Part of minding your own business is knowing when to stay out of things that don't involve you. But it also means taking responsibility for things that do. Every able-minded human with a heartbeat should find some way to contribute to the fight against this evil. This isn't something that is just happening overseas. This is happening in our own backyard. Our shopping malls, our fast-food restaurants, our nail salons. That makes it our business. At the bare minimum, you should do your part to educate yourself and help educate people within your circle of influence, especially children. If you are a parent, then this applies directly to you. I'll give more specific thoughts on this subject in just a few minutes.

There are times to butt out of a situation and there are times to get involved. This is happening on our soil to children like yours and like mine. That makes it our fucking business and we need to mind it.

HOLD YOURSELF TO THE SAME OR HIGHER STANDARD AS YOU HOLD OTHERS TO

One of the only ways that we will take down the powerful individuals in high places responsible for keeping this industry alive is by people having the balls and willingness to call out their own. People are quick to crucify the guy on the other side when reports of wrongdoing come out. But these cries usually get chalked up to partisanism or hate. We need more upstanding citizens who are willing to *call out their own.*

If proof surfaces that a political figure from *your political party* committed a criminal act or sexual offense, *call them out.* If a pastor from your religious faith is convicted of sexually abusing children, *call them out.* If a figure from your favorite sports team is exposed and proven guilty for raping someone, *call them out.* We need strong voices who hold themselves, and *those they align with*, to a higher standard. We need more people unwilling to tolerate, cover up, or look the other way when the people in power are proven to be involved in criminal acts.

While there are many angles we could look at this issue from and more complexities to the approaches for putting a stop to it, I'll summarize the solution to this problem with three things:

1. Diminish demand by making consequences so high that it deters the purchaser.
2. Crush supply by empowering law enforcement with tools and resources to help them in catching and apprehending traffickers.
3. Educate and empower our society to know what to look for and speak up when something isn't right.

As always, I'll wrap up by sharing a few actionable things that you can do to contribute to positive change in regard to this issue.

VOTE FOR THE RIGHT PEOPLE FOR THE RIGHT REASONS

As an American citizen, you are given the opportunity to play a role in the process of electing the most powerful political figures in our nation. Do not take this lightly. It is imperative that every person does their part to make sure that we are voting for individuals with strong moral character. It is imperative that we do not tolerate criminal scandals and proven sexual offenses in the lives of our leaders. Do not look the other way simply because someone is the frontrunner of your political party. Do not vote for someone because you like them marginally better than the other guy. And do not cast a vote based solely on judiciary implication.

BE AN INFORMED PARENT WHO PROTECTS
AND PREPARES THEIR CHILDREN

One of the greatest things that the everyday citizen can do is to prepare and protect their children. This begins by educating yourself as an individual. Do your research. Learn what you need to be on the lookout for and how best to prepare your children. Then sit down and have the necessary conversations with them. The point is not to instill fear or paranoia, but rather to empower them with knowledge and a basic understanding of the best courses of action to take in various dangerous situations.

It's also incredibly important to teach your children how to spot warning signs in their friends and peers. Children don't always listen to their parents and they don't always give their parents the full story. The older a child gets, the more the parents may find themselves excluded from certain aspects of a child's life. But, more often than not, they have a friend. Or a few friends. Friends who know their secrets. Friends who know where they hang out. Friends who know about their latest romantic fling or flame. Friends who would know if something was off if they were properly armed with knowing what to look for. We need to teach kids how to react if they are placed in certain situations and the warning signs that something isn't right with one of their friends. Parents would also be wise to stay current with other parents. With more information on the whereabouts of children and the ability to compare notes, a much fuller picture can be provided as to the child's safety.

Technology can also be a great tool for parents. It gives parents the ability to check in with their children and also track the child's location through any number of apps. A location tracker can be used until the parent feels that *they* have done a sufficient job in their parenting to prepare the child enough to be fully trusted to make smart choices. Once that level of maturity is reached, and the parent feels comfortable, the parent can eliminate the need for tracking.

Informing and educating society on this issue is something that deserves federal attention and funding. From speakers in schools, to educational materials, to resources devoted to helping empower parents, the possibilities are endless as to how more awareness could be brought to this issue on a national and international level.

CONTRIBUTE TO THOSE DOING GOOD

As awareness for this problem grows, numerous nonprofit organizations and efforts are popping up to fight this from all sides. There are organizations dedicated to providing top-of-the-line technology and training for law enforcement to aid in catching traffickers and purchasers. There are nonprofits that provide safe homes to help victims recover from trauma and create a new life. There are efforts to help educate and inform people on the warning signs of danger so that bad situations can be avoided. If you are looking for ways to make a bigger contribution to eradicating this problem, a little research will quickly connect you with the efforts and organizations in your area that are doing good work. These organizations could always use more willing hands or funds. Depending on the type of organization, there may be an opportunity for you to donate time, expertise, or resources to the effort.

HAVE THE UNCOMFORTABLE CONVERSATION WITH YOURSELF

In closing, I want to urge you to force yourself to have the uncomfortable conversation that we discussed earlier in this chapter about whether or not you're prepared to do what it takes to put a stop to this evil. Our nation needs to have a collective come-to-Jesus moment, take a hard look in the mirror, and ask ourselves just how serious we are about fighting this thing. Individuals need to take the time to dig deep and see what they are willing to do to protect the innocent.

Every man and woman who has come face-to-face with war and the harsh realities of active combat has been forced to grapple with this. The American people enjoy their liberty and way of life because there are those willing to take the necessary steps to protect our freedom and fight against any force that threatens it. There are evils in this world that will not be stopped by more sympathetic appeals, more love and compassion, more awareness, and more candlelight vigils. Some evil will only be crushed through swift, severe action. Very few people want to be the tip of that spear, but someone has to do it. So I will leave you with these two questions once again:

How much do you want this to end?

And are you willing to do what's necessary to protect the innocent?

CHAPTER 11

★

SOCIAL ISSUES

The next thing I'd like to put on the table for discussion is a handful of social issues that need to be talked about. There are many that could be discussed but we will primarily focus on drugs, healthcare, LGBTQ rights, and abortion. While these topics are very different in some respects, there is one way in which they are all the same: *they all have to do with choices people make that others do not agree with.*

There are some people who want to do a line of blow in their apartment and others who strongly oppose that choice. There are some people who believe that a woman should have the right to choose whether or not she'd like to be pregnant and others who believe that the act of abortion is child murder. There are some people who'd like to marry someone of the same sex and others who believe that homosexual matrimony will destroy the sanctity of marriage.

We will dive into each issue individually, but there are a couple of things that I think are important to get clear on before we jump in. First and foremost, it's important to *remember the purpose of our government.*

- It is *not* the job of the government to ensure that we are healthy, wealthy, or happy.

- It *is* the job of the government to protect the rights of its citizens so that every individual is given the *opportunity* to make themselves any of those things.

- It is not the role of the government to legislate good behavior, kindness, politeness, or behaviors that fall in line with a particular religion. We live in a free country and that means that each individual is given the freedom to live their life and make choices as they see fit *so long as it does not directly harm others.*

The very foundation of our government revolves around protecting freedom in all aspects of life—from speech, to religion, to assembly, to bearing arms. *Freedom and liberty are easy to support when everyone agrees with what everyone else is doing, saying, and choosing.* It's when we *don't* agree with what someone else is doing, saying, and choosing that laws become very important to have in place in order to protect our freedom and rights.

Secondly, I think it's very important to remember that while there are many elements of Judeo-Christian values that were woven into our history and government, one of the cornerstone principles that our nation was founded upon was the separation of church and state. Anyone who's read a fourth-grade history book knows that a desire for freedom of religion was one of the greatest motivations behind many of America's first settlements. I think it's incredibly important that we stand by this as a nation. To make something illegal simply because your religion does not agree with it flies in the face of the very freedoms our nation was built upon. And anyone who has been placed in a position of power and authority in our government should hold to this principle. *It is wrong for **any** government authority to seek to enforce their religious beliefs or set of personal preferences on others.*

As an individual, it is your right to practice your faith and religion as you see fit. It is your right to dislike and disagree with the choices of others based upon those beliefs. If you want to live your life by the Bible, that is your right. But the Constitution is our nation's bible. And just as the Christian religion is driven by their Bible, our nation and its policies should be driven by ours. Our laws *should* revolve around ensuring and protecting every citizen's rights and freedoms. Our laws *should not* seek to enforce any set of religious principles or legislate good behaviors.

You should be free to live your life as you wish, so long as it does not directly harm anyone else. And if you make poor choices that yield tough consequences, you alone should be responsible to bear them. The government should not have to pick up the pieces, bail you out, or lend you a hand while you face the negative effects of your own poor choices. That's your burden, and your burden alone, to bear.

If someone makes a choice that *you disagree with* but that does not cause direct harm to you or anyone else, it's none of your damn business. It's their life and they should be able to choose what they want. That's what it means to live in a free country. It's as simple as that. We'll break down how this plays out in each of the specific topics below. As with every other topic that we've opened, we'll use the same four principles to unpack and assess these issues.

DRUGS

I think it's safe to assume that the majority of American citizens do not want to live in a society riddled by the presence of drugs. The process of producing, trafficking, and distributing illegal drugs creates a number of harmful effects on the public. I shared quite a few disturbing statistics in the first chapter that shed light on just how rampant the drug problem is in our society. As a result, there have been many attempts and efforts made to eradicate this problem. It obviously hasn't done much to help. Drugs are as prevalent as ever. It's a dark trade that operates in the shadows—thriving in the underbelly of illegalities.

To better assess this issue, we'll implement our four principles so we can get a better handle on how to approach it logically.

Remove Emotions

It doesn't take long to find heartbreaking stories about lives that the effects of excessive drug use have wrecked. We've all seen the haunting, gaunt images of faces enslaved by the demands of addiction. These cause us to feel sad and angry. No one wants their child to be an addict. No one wants to watch a loved one's life implode because of drugs. It makes us want to take action and do something to get rid of this problem for good. But as we've discussed before, emotions must be removed in order to assess the issue at hand reasonably.

Many efforts have been made to solve the drug problem in America. Some efforts focus on shutting down manufacturing. Others try to catch drugs in transit along the route into the United States or across state lines. Others focus on trying to stop distribution. Others target apprehending the user.

But one thing is for sure. *None of it seems to be working.*

To me, as with human trafficking, I think the solution lies in finding a way to *extinguish demand, not supply.* However, *unlike* human trafficking, the use of drugs does not directly, in and of itself, involve harming another human being. Therefore, in my opinion, the choice to alter one's state of mind through the use of drugs shouldn't be illegal. If someone wants to snort a line of cocaine in his bathroom or get high while she watches a sitcom, I think it should be their right to do so. I don't like it. I wouldn't do it. I don't agree with it. But I don't think the act of altering oneself through drugs should be illegal in and of itself. And here's why.

By making drugs illegal, it only incentivizes the creation of a black market. It promotes illegal activity. And it's obvious that it's been ineffective. Take a look at how the Prohibition movement worked out. It was motivated by a seemingly good cause: to bring American families back together, reduce alcoholism, and promote good morals and behavior. It actually pushed alcohol into the underbelly of the black market and created a whole new set of problems. When alcohol was once again legalized, the demand that fueled the black market for alcohol disappeared. The law stopped focusing on the act of drinking alcohol and instead targeted illegal actions made by individuals that were harmful to others such as drinking and driving, assault, or the destruction of property.

The same could be applied to drugs. By legalizing drugs across the board, we could eliminate the black market and all of the illegal activity that is brought into society as a result. The entire industry is a playground for corruption, manipulation, exploitation, and crime. While this may sound like an extreme position, the unsettling truth that most Americans refuse to face is this: *Drugs will be sold, purchased, and used whether they are legal or not. It's only our denial of that fact that allows a crime-filled black market to thrive on our streets.*

Having said that, I also believe that there should be *swift and severe consequences* given to people who harm others in any way. I don't care if you're tripped out on drugs or not, if you hit someone with your car, or assault someone, or abuse a child, you should suffer consequences for that. No one should feel sorry for you if your ass is sitting in jail or if you get your driver's license taken away. You can't blame the substance for your action any more than you can blame a firearm for murdering someone. Every individual should be held responsible for their actions that cause harm to others. And the consequences of those actions should be harsh and exacting.

Eventually, society will learn that though they have the freedom to purchase and partake of drugs, it is not always wise or profitable to do so. If consequences are severe enough, people will think twice before partaking in a substance that could alter their abilities to make good choices.

Remove Politics

When it comes to an issue like drugs, it's easy to want the government to come in and act as a protective parent, babysitting its citizens and making sure that they don't harm their bodies or destroy their lives. But again, *that's not the role of the government.* Science proves that excess sugar and too much fast food also harm the body, but no one is moving to outlaw hamburgers and ice cream. There are many politicians who promote the idea that we need *more* government, *more* laws, and *more* oversight to help people behave in a way that will yield a happier, healthier, friendlier society. While it may sound like a good idea, it's not. To quote Benjamin Franklin, "They who can give up essential liberty to obtain a little temporary safety, deserve neither liberty nor safety."

We *cannot* give up our liberties in hopes that the government will create a perfect society. This thinking leads down a road that will eventually destroy the very freedom and way of life that we hold so dear.

Mind Your Own Fucking Business

I don't like drugs. I don't do drugs. I will do everything in my power to raise children who aren't chronic drug users. I think most of them are harmful to the body and have detrimental effects on the mind. But at the end of the day, what someone does on their own time is none of my business. If there's a crazy motherfucker out there who wants to drink paint or sniff gasoline, it's not my job or yours to stop them. Once someone is a functioning adult, they should have the freedom to make their own choices as long as it doesn't hurt or harm anyone. I don't have to like it and neither do you. But if we want to be able to live our lives as we see fit as long as it doesn't hurt anyone, then we must mind our own business and allow others to do the same.

Hold Yourself to the Same or Higher Standard as You Hold Others To

If you want to live in a world with less drug use, I think it's important to ask yourselves, *why is there such a demand for this?* While I don't think it's the role of the government to control the demand, it's certainly a worthy conversation for our society to have as to why so many people have such a need to live in an altered state of mind. It's something that parents especially should be having conversations about—with other parents, with experts, and with their children. If we want to see a change in society, we, as individuals, need to start taking responsibility to do everything we can to educate, prepare, and raise the next generation.

HEALTHCARE

It doesn't take a genius to recognize that there are some real problems with our healthcare system. Flip back to the statistics I highlighted in the first chapter and skim over them again if you need to. One thing is abundantly clear: Americans are growing unhealthier by the day and it's costing this country a fortune. The scary truth is that there is no mathematical equation, policy, or initiative that can solve a problem in which there are more sick, overweight, unhealthy people in need of regular healthcare than not. There is simply no way to sustain this. Insurance, irrespective of industry, hinges upon the fact that there are more paying in than are using it. Once there are more people using it than paying for it, we've got a real problem on our hands. Let's apply our four principles here as well.

Remove Emotion

I'm just going to say it. Fatassery is a problem in our nation. But somehow obesity, out of all the health issues that people face, has become a sensitive subject that people tiptoe around for fear of hurting someone's feelings. But the truth is that if you are obese, your risk for a whole host of health issues skyrockets. A massive portion of healthcare costs could be avoided by people making simple, consistent, healthy lifestyle choices.

Dr. Mark Hyman, the Head of Strategy and Innovation of the Cleveland Clinic Center for Functional Medicine, a thirteen-time *New York Times* bestselling author, and Board President for Clinical Affairs for the Institute for Functional Medicine and leading expert on the subject of health and its impact on our nation and economy, states:

> Seventy percent of annual deaths in the US are caused by chronic diseases. These preventable conditions are also the leading cause of disability and they're everywhere. The facts are pretty startling: *six in ten adults have a chronic disease and we now know that the economic burden of these amounts to more than $1 trillion annually.*
>
> Let that sink in—our country is spending more than $1 trillion every single year on diseases that could be prevented through the right lifestyle choices. Heart disease, hypertension, stroke, type 2 diabetes, obesity, and cancer are just some of the many diseases we know can be prevented and treated using interventions like good nutrition, exercise, stress reduction, and high-quality sleep.
>
> Not only would public health benefit from a focus on prevention of chronic disease using these tools, but the economy would hugely benefit as well. For example, the Milken Institute estimates that with the right efforts *we could avoid 40 million cases of chronic disease* by 2023 and reduce the economic burden by 27 percent. Looking at obesity alone, declining rates could save the country $60 billion in treatment costs."[33]

---

33 Mark Hyman, "How Disease Impacts the Economy." *Dr. Mark Hyman*, October 18, 2019, https://drhyman.com/blog/2019/05/09/how-disease-impacts-the-economy/.

I'm sorry this hurts your feelings, but if you are overweight and sitting at home, literally eating yourself sick because you have no willpower, while the rest of us pay to prevent you from feeling the detrimental effects of *your own choices*...that's fucking ridiculous and you're a selfish asshole. If you think that you're not hurting anyone else with your choice not to do simple things to care for yourself, you're just plain wrong. You're bending over those who have legitimate, non-self-induced medical issues by taking time and resources. And financially you're screwing us all because your health issues contribute significantly to increased premiums and deductibles.

Obesity is a real issue in our country and we've got to remove emotions, stop beating around the bush, and stop worrying more about someone feeling "fat-shamed" than the long-term health of our people. We've got to start talking about the elephant in the room when it comes to healthcare, which is the fact that *the power to solve the healthcare crisis lies in the hands of individuals*. While there are some health issues that arise suddenly and are unavoidable, there are *many* health issues that can be completely avoided by simply making solid, healthy choices in regard to what we put in our mouth and how we move our bodies.

If you've had three bypass surgeries because you're 450 pounds and you're unwilling to move your fat ass or lay off the French fries and pizza, the rest of us shouldn't have to shoulder the consequences of your lack of willpower. Maybe it sounds unfeeling or mean, but it's not. It's absolutely logical and fair. If you want to party and play video games all day and not work, that's your prerogative. But I'm not going to pay off your debt or give you free rent when you end up homeless.

Simply put, emergency medicine should be a right. Anytime, anywhere, no matter what your social standing or financial situation. But healthcare costs associated with *preventable discomforts and conditions* should be the responsibility of the individual who refused to make the simple choices that would nullify the need for that medical care in the first place.

As a society, we've got to stop worrying so much about making people feel bad about themselves, hurting feelings, or stepping on toes and face this rampant problem head-on.

Remove Politics

There are many political agendas that have made their way into our food industry and medical care system. There is an incredible amount of money wrapped up in both systems. And where there's money, you can bet there will be corruption. I'm not going to get into the ins and outs of these issues; that could be a book in and of itself. But I will say this: *educate yourself.* Do your own research. Don't be quickly influenced by the media. Don't spout party lines. And don't assume to oppose something because you dislike the person heading up the effort.

Take time to remove political biases and educate yourself on the issues at play in our food industry and medical system. Because you're naive if you think there isn't both corruption and a dangerous agenda woven throughout both.

Mind Your Own Fucking Business

While I believe that obesity and preventable diseases are a huge expense to our nation, I don't think the government should take away someone's hamburger or outlaw ice cream. It's not the food's fault that people are in the state they are in, it's theirs. If you're a grown adult, you get to choose what you put in your mouth. Nobody is force-feeding you. While our food industry could use some help and there are certain areas in our nation with less access to healthy ingredients, just about everyone can get their hands on decently nutritious foods and choose to eat them. Anyone can quit guzzling sugar-filled drinks. Anyone can stand on their own two feet and go for a jog or do some fucking air squats and jumping jacks. It's not complicated. It's not rocket science.

So if you make the choice to sit on your ass all day, binge eat, and watch Netflix by night, that's your choice and your right. I'll mind my business and live my life the way I see fit and you can mind yours. But if *your* choices cause *your* body to be unhealthy and in need of expensive medical treatment, that should be *your problem, not mine.* The rest of us who make an effort to have healthy bodies shouldn't have to bear the burden of others who don't. It shouldn't be up to us to foot the bill of the medical costs associated with your poor behaviors.

Part of minding your own business is shouldering the costs of your lifestyle. You made the choice and if it's a costly and expensive one, that's yours to deal with.

That's why I think there's nothing wrong with rates being determined by each individual's health as it pertains to preventable diseases and conditions. If you have a genetic condition or unavoidable disease, that should be covered. But if you want insurance companies to shell out thousands of dollars to cushion the discomfort of your sedentary, overweight lifestyle without you paying an extra dime...

...then fuck you.

Hold Yourself to the Same or Higher Standard as You Hold Others To

The only way we're going to solve the healthcare crisis is if individuals step up to the plate and take some personal responsibility. We've got to break the cycle of people making poor decisions and refusing to hold themselves accountable or feel any consequence for their choices.

Think of it this way: If you're driving a fully insured rental car, you won't feel the need to take care of it the way you'd take care of one you purchased with your own hard-earned cash. If you know that someone else will pay for every ding, scratch, and spill you put the vehicle through, you won't feel any pressure to make sure that it's well taken care of. In the same manner, your body, when guaranteed total insurance as it pertains to all expenses associated with your health, is essentially a rental car. You will continue to make careless choices if you know that you can beat the fucking shit out of it and then just ask for a pill to help with your high blood pressure, insulin, sleep problems, low testosterone, depressed mood, aches and pains, and whatever else has been caused by your self-inflicted unhealthy state.

On the converse, if you know that all medical costs associated with preventable discomforts, ailments, and diseases are coming out of your pocket, you might just feel some incentive to order the salad or go for a run or stay away from things that could harm you. If you know that you are responsible for bearing the burden of your lifestyle, you better believe you're going to take care of yourself. It's not right to play the victim and cry out for better healthcare while you abuse your body every day and refuse to take responsibility for it. As a society, it is imperative that we take a collective look in the mirror and hold ourselves accountable for the things that are within our power to change.

ABORTION

This is another issue that is surrounded by vehement disagreement and opposing positions.

You've got people on one side who say that every woman should have the right to choose what takes place inside her own body. You've got people on the other side who say that abortion is the slaughter of innocent children. You already know where we're going to start.

Remove Emotion

The pro-life movement has introduced a whole host of emotions into this discussion with the claim that anyone who has an abortion or even supports it is a child murderer. This makes it nearly impossible to have a rational discussion about the issues. That's why we need to approach this logically and look at what science has to say on the subject.

There is a point at which life begins. A time when a living, breathing, individual human with its own set of rights takes its place in our world. I believe that line is determined by nature. When nature sees fit to push a fetus out into the world and that fetus takes its first breath and organs begin functioning on their own, unattached to anything else, nature declares it an individual human being. Before that, when it is a fetus still in utero, it is part of a woman's body. As such, a woman should have full autonomy to make choices for her own body, including terminating an unwanted pregnancy.

The pro-life movement has used their religious beliefs about when life begins to inform their outlook on this issue (which we'll discuss more in a moment). They believe that life begins at conception, thus making the termination of a pregnancy murder in their eyes. Based upon this belief, the pro-life movement has employed many emotion-inducing tactics to push people into adopting their beliefs on the subject. The topic of partial-birth abortions is often brought into the discussion from the pro-life movement, making it sound as if this is something that is happening constantly. So let's take a look at the data.

According to the Alan Guttmacher Institute, an abortion-rights research group that conducts surveys of the nation's abortion doctors, about 15,000 abortions were performed on women twenty weeks or more along in their pregnancies; the vast majority were between the twentieth and twenty-fourth week. Of those, only about 2,200 D&X (a "dilation and extraction" method developed by a doctor to extract a fetus intact, typically used after twenty weeks of pregnancy) abortions were performed, or about 0.2 percent of the 1.3 million abortions believed to be performed that year. Contrary to the claims of some abortion opponents, most such abortions do not take place in the third trimester of pregnancy, or after fetal "viability."

Although 0.2 percent of 1.3 million abortions is not a lot, these statistics separate fact from fiction and feeling. Many of the emotion-eliciting stories and "facts" used by those who take a pro-life stance are simply inaccurate. Science says that when a fetus is ready to live, thrive, and function on its own, it's a human life with rights that should be protected. Before that moment, a fetus is an extension of a woman's body and it's her right to do what she wants to do with her body. Whether or not you agree with her choice is irrelevant.[34]

Remove Politics

My stance on abortion may come as a surprise to some who've mistakenly boxed me into a set of political beliefs that align with a particular political party. It's very important to me to assess every issue individually.

In my opinion, religion has played a huge part in influencing the position of politicians who, in turn, influence people and policy. As we discussed before, we must uphold the separation of church and state. *This means that religious beliefs cannot and should not influence the position of our nation's laws.* The Constitution is the *only* bible that we should cling to.

---

34 Julie Rovner, "'Partial-Birth Abortion': Separating Fact From Spin," *NPR*, February 22, 2006, https://www.npr.org/2006/02/21/5168163/partial-birth-abortion-separating-fact-from-spin.

This issue should *not* be dictated by politicians with their own personal, religious leanings or influenced by the desire to cater to people with certain religious positions. This is one way that politics must be removed. Additionally, I think it's important for each individual to assess this issue on its own, instead of assuming to take a position based upon the beliefs of one particular political party.

Mind Your Own Fucking Business

If you believe that life begins at conception and want to live your own life accordingly, that's okay. If you believe that abortion is a sin because of your religious beliefs and live your own life accordingly, that's okay as well. But that doesn't mean that the entire country should be forced to adopt your religious beliefs. It doesn't mean that everyone should have your views regarding when life begins. Those are your beliefs and you are welcome to make choices based upon them. Have your beliefs, live your life, and then mind your own fucking business instead of trying to force your personal religion and views on the entire public.

It's also important to understand that the same freedom that gives you the liberty to practice your religion as you see fit also affords others the freedom *not to hold* your same views. To want freedom for yourself and then force your religious beliefs on others is just plain hypocrisy. You can't have it both ways. Remember, the laws that protect our freedom are most important when we *don't* agree on a subject.

Hold Yourself to the Same or Higher Standard as You Hold Others to

The last thing that I'd like to add on this subject has to do with the financial responsibility to care for a child. If we are going to support the right to choose, this must be practiced across the board. As a society, if we are going to uphold "my body, my choice," then individuals should be ready to accept all the consequences and responsibilities for their personal choice to terminate a pregnancy or to bring the pregnancy to full term and have a baby.

Let's say that a man and woman have sex and it results in pregnancy. Upon hearing this news, the man makes it clear that he *does not* want to be a father. Perhaps he does not feel financially prepared to do so. Perhaps he does not want children at all. Whatever the case may be, he makes it clear to the woman that he does not feel that he is in a position to be a father. She makes the decision to carry to term and have a baby.

At this point in time, I believe that it's unfair for the woman to force her choice on the man and make him financially responsible for the child that she chose to bring into the world. If we're going to support the right to choose, that should be given to both the mother and the father. If, as a society, we have agreed to view pregnancy as optional, then that option should be given to both the man and the woman. If a man doesn't want to be a father and the woman decides to go ahead and be a mother, that is her choice, but that should mean that she relinquishes her rights to force the man to bear the responsibilities of that choice, financially or otherwise.

If the man and woman both agree to have a child together and accept that responsibility, then both should be responsible for the child in every way. A contract would make this entire process simple. If a woman is pregnant and informs the man, he can choose to sign a contract that says that he is in support of having the baby and therefore accepts responsibility for it or he can sign over complete rights to the woman if he is *not* in favor of carrying the pregnancy to term and having a child. In the case that a man wants to have a baby and the woman *does not* want to have a baby, the decision should ultimately lay in the hands of the woman because growing the fetus to term and delivering it involves her body. Perhaps it seems unfair to the man, but that's simply the hand nature dealt.

It's important that we seek to uphold freedom and the right to choose across the board in regard to this issue. We must uphold freedom by not forcing one set of religious beliefs on the public. We must also support the right to choose by giving both the man and the woman a say in the matter and allowing each woman to decide what is best for her and her body.

LGBTQ RIGHTS

I'd like to talk a little bit about LGBTQ rights. There has been a lot of conversation around this subject in recent years, and it is often brought up under the heading of social issues. We'll use our four principles here as well.

Remove Emotion

When it comes to same-sex marriage, it's hard for me to understand why this is still a point of contention. If two consenting adults want to enter into a marriage with one another and build a life together, they should absolutely be allowed to.

There are some who say that same sex marriage "destroys the sanctity of marriage," and to those people I'd like to say that if Kim Kardashian hasn't done that already, gay marriage sure as hell isn't going to. Also, what about the divorce and infidelity rates in our nation? If you want to uphold some idyllic idea of marriage, then to me, that should be talked about long before whether or not two people of the same sex can legally marry. It's absurd. Just because your religious beliefs cause you to see same-sex marriage as a sin does not mean that *anyone* else should hold that belief. And it does not mean that laws should be created around it. Same-sex marriage should be legalized across the board. End of story.

Before moving on, however, I'd like to talk a little bit about transgender issues while we're working on removing emotions. This is a topic in which it is *vital* to set aside emotions before assessing. We must approach it logically and without sensitive feelings and emotions that cloud our perspective.

I find it baffling that oftentimes the very same people who are on "team science" and in support of abortion from a biological perspective suddenly throw science right out the window when it comes to transgender issues. The basis of the human race relies upon reproduction, which requires sexual organs. In the simplest terms, if you have the ability to create and produce eggs, you are a female. If you are born with the ability to create and produce sperm, you are a male. This divides the population, biologically, into two categories. This is not my personal belief; it is simply a scientific fact.

If an individual decides to alter their hormones, physical appearance, and genitalia, that is absolutely their prerogative. If an individual wants to request that a different pronoun be used when others refer to them, that is also their prerogative. If you were born with a penis and want it removed and a vagina put in its place, breasts added to your chest area, and to wear women's clothing, that's fine. That choice has no bearing on anyone's life but your own. It's a free country. Your choices for your body and how you'd like to relate to yourself are your business.

With transgender issues, however, there are aspects that *do* begin affecting others when it comes to topics such as sporting events. There's been a lot of talk lately about where transgender people fit into sports leagues that are divided into male and female categories. To me, these should be divided by the biological sex of the individual at birth. If the individual was born with the ability to create and produce sperm, then that individual should compete in the male division, regardless of whether or not they have chosen to alter their body or relate to themselves as something besides a male. If the individual was born with the ability to create and produce eggs, they should compete in the female division regardless of whether or not they have chosen to alter their body or relate to themselves as something besides a female.

Why? Because sports involve other people. Just because you don't choose to identify with the biological designation you were born with does not mean that others should be affected by that choice. If there is an individual who was born with the ability to create and produce sperm who wakes up one day and decides that they'd like to identify as a female, that's fine. But if that individual then wants to compete in female sporting leagues as a female, this choice would directly impact the female athletes in that division. Therefore, this should not be allowed. We must side with science, not personal belief and preference, when it comes to implementing rules for the public to abide by.

Remove Politics

When it comes to politics and LGBTQ rights, as with abortion, it is important that our politicians uphold the Constitution and freedom and refrain from allowing their personal religious views to cloud their leadership, judgment, or policy creation.

Additionally, this issue is a classic example of people wanting the government to step in and legislate good behaviors and polite manners. There has been a lot of talk about "hate speech" as stories are circulated about rude remarks made toward the LGBTQ community. Many people are crying out for the government to step in and form legislation to stop this kind of behavior.

I believe that's a mistake. Once you start legislating "being offended," questions arise as to what's off-limits and what isn't and who decides which is which. This whole notion of censoring or legislating rude behaviors is a slippery slope that we would be wise to avoid completely. Otherwise, we will find ourselves infringing on our freedom of speech, which is a cornerstone of our nation's very foundation. Criminalizing hate speech gets a ball rolling that can't be stopped. One person's "hate speech" is another person's idea of a sarcastic joke. Once you allow people's feelings to dictate the law, you've created a dangerous situation.

Guess what? Shitty people are going to say shitty things sometimes. People are going to be homophobic, racist, sexist, and just plain fucking mean. I don't like it. I wish it wasn't like that. Unfortunately, people are just assholes sometimes and it shouldn't be the job of the government to teach people manners or how to speak politely. We need to keep politics out of it.

If you want to live in a world where people don't make fun of other people, guess what you can do? Be someone who doesn't fucking make fun of people and raise kids who don't either. That's how we change as a society. It's about individuals taking responsibility to better *themselves* and set an example instead of playing the victim and crying out for the government to teach some assholes with a big mouth a lesson.

Mind Your Own Fucking Business

Minding your own fucking business is more or less the theme of this entire section. If someone wants to marry someone of the same sex, why the hell should it bother you? *Mind your own fucking business.*

If you'd like to ask someone to refer to you as he, she, or Ze, you're more than free to. The other person is also free to comply or not comply with your request. At the end of the day, if you disagree, each of you should *mind your own fucking business* and carry on with your lives.

If you think same-sex marriage is a sinful act because of your religious beliefs, then believe what you believe, *mind your own fucking business*, and let the rest of society live their own goddamn lives in peace.

If everyone would stay in their lane, respect each other's differences, and support every individual's right to live their lives as they see fit, so long as it doesn't harm anyone else, we wouldn't even have anything to discuss here.

Hold Yourself to the Same or Higher Standard as You Hold Others to
It is a double standard to want the freedom to carry a gun while simultaneously wishing to control someone else's right to marry whomever they want. It's also a double standard to stand behind biology when it comes to a women's right to choose and then throw it out when it comes to transgender athletes.

Across the board, more people need to take a look in the mirror and hold themselves to the same or higher standard as they hold everyone else to.

In the vein of supporting total freedom of choice across the board, whether that relates to abortion or your view of your sexuality or anything else we've discussed, I believe that business owners should be given that same freedom. If a business owner does not want to bake a cake for a same-sex wedding, it's his or her right to refuse. If a business owner terminates the employment of one of his workers because they are transgender, that's also his or her right. If a business owner is racist, sexist, homophobic, or hates people with mustaches and makes decisions in regard to his or her business accordingly, that's their right.

In previous times in our history, when discrimination was rampant, we needed more policies and laws in place to protect minority groups. But society has come a long way since then.

In an age where information can be made public in an instant and racism, sexism, and discrimination are hated with a passion, one tweet, Facebook post, or video upload to YouTube can expose the deeds of an disreputable business owner to the entire world.

To me, issues like this shouldn't be solved by attempting to make poor behavior legal or illegal. Issues like this are solved by society when the masses dole out punishment by withdrawing support from businesses with poor practices. So rather than wanting the law to force a baker to make a cake for a same-sex wedding begrudgingly, why not instead expose their refusal and let the public put them out of business? Which one do you think teaches a more severe lesson?

If you lose a job because you're gay, let society be outraged, withdraw support, and kick them to the curb. If you don't think a company has good business practices, then start your own fucking company and run them out of business. If you see a business with practices you don't agree with, don't support them with your money.

At the heart of all of these issues is this fact: if we are going to uphold freedom, we must do so consistently across the board. You can't ask for the government to give you freedom for the things *you agree with* and control and outlaw the things *you don't*. You simply can't have it both ways. You must hold yourself to the same or higher standard than you hold others to.

Whether we're talking about drugs, abortion, healthcare, or LGBTQ rights, there are four simple things that you, as an individual, can do in regard to this issue:

1. Educate yourself.
2. Make up your own damn mind about each issue without being influenced by politics.
3. Challenge yourself to eradicate hypocrisy within your own belief system.
4. Lead by example and vote with your wallet.

CHAPTER 12

★

THE ECONOMY

There are few things that impact the day-to-day lives of the American people as much as the economy. No matter who you are or what job you have, your life is touched and affected by the economy every single day. Since the beginning, our nation has been known as the land of opportunity—and with good reason. There is no shortage of opportunity here. We are a land where immigrants can build empires. Where children born into poverty can become leaders in our government. Where anyone and everyone is given a shot at building the life they dream of and desire. It's certainly not perfect. People deal with setbacks and obstacles just as all humans do. Still, our nation abounds with stories of people from every kind of situation, background, and ability achieving greatness and becoming wildly successful. This is one of the most remarkable aspects of what it means to be an American citizen.

But if we hope to continue this way of life, we *must* protect our economy and free market. The more robust our economy and market, the more opportunity will abound—giving this generation and the one to come the chance for great success.

That's why this topic is so important to discuss. But have you ever noticed that when the subject of "the economy" comes up in conversation, it is quickly met with the attitude that it's a topic that is too hard, complex, and intricate for the everyday person to understand? We are told that only experts understand it, that only *they* can break it down into terms that are intelligible to an average person.

I think that's bullshit. And honestly a bit of a cop-out.

This big smoke-and-mirrors, lights-and-pony-tricks fanfare around the "complexities" of our nation's economy is oftentimes nothing more than a way to pull the wool over the American people's eyes so that they won't notice that they are getting fucked over. There is no reason that this subject should be so complicated and convoluted. There are straightforward and logical solutions to many of the problems we face if we would let the blinders fall away. So let's dive in.

REMOVE EMOTIONS

Many of the issues surrounding the topic of our economy exist because people's emotions have been polluted and have convoluted their ability to make logical assessments. When you have a free market system and give individuals the *opportunity* to create wealth and success, you will always have people who find a way to seize that opportunity and use it for a positive outcome and those who don't. You are going to have people with a little, people with some, and people with a lot.

Problems arise when the people with a little feel slighted by the people with a lot and the people with a lot feel bad about it. They feel guilty and sorry for the fact that they have more and begin to believe that it's their job to correct the system so that everyone is ensured an equal *outcome.* In this seemingly good and righteous pursuit, overcorrection is almost inevitable and collateral damage ensues. This leads to a complete swing in the opposite direction, creating a whole new set of problems that are actually far worse.

We cannot base our economic system upon emotions and sympathy. One of the greatest reasons our nation has achieved such a level of success is because of the power of capitalism. Capitalism is defined as *"an economic and political system in which a country's trade and industry are controlled by private owners for profit, rather than by the state."* In this environment, every individual has a shot at wild success. Billion-dollar companies are started in garages. Single moms who lived out of their cars build empires. High school dropouts innovate the next technological breakthrough. Anyone has the chance to make something of themselves. Of course there are losses as well. Small businesses have to shut down when larger ones capture their clientele. People go bankrupt. Good people experience hard losses.

The truth is that everyone's life, financial situation, and level of success is going to look a little bit different. This is a fact of life. But some people don't like it. They feel bad about it.

If someone has a lot and someone has a little, shouldn't we take from one person and give it to the other?

Shouldn't we make things even and fair across the board?

Shouldn't we give more help, support, and handouts to those who don't have much?

Shouldn't we want every person to have a fair and equal outcome in life?

Perhaps these sentiments seem noble. In reality, they are the dump truck that is pouring the asphalt of good intentions, paving the road straight to hell.

We must abolish the thinking that one person's success means that someone else was slighted. There is not a finite amount of money or opportunity in this world. One person's increase does not necessarily mean another must decrease.

The moment you give handouts to every person, irrespective of their work, is the moment you extinguish the deep hunger in the bellies of individuals who would give everything to achieve success.

If you give a lion in the jungle a platter of fresh meat every day, he will cease to hunt. If he can nap all day and still enjoy the exact same outcome, why would he bother himself? And as the other lions watch him eating his fresh meat every day without lifting a paw, suddenly the desire to go farther into the jungle, to pursue their prey, to struggle for that next meal seems irrelevant. Why not sit at the edge of the forest and ask for a piece of the handout? Why work so hard?

The opportunity to both achieve and fail, to become a great success or an epic failure, is what creates the passion, drive, fervor, and fury that pushes individuals to strive for greatness. Whether or not we always accomplish everything we desire, it's the knowledge that there is always more opportunity that keeps us pushing our limits. It keeps us innovating, creating, and holding onto hope that every day is a new chance to become more than we were the day before. This environment has birthed the greatest advancements, discoveries, inventions, and innovations of our time. *And we cannot allow misguided empathy to destroy that.*

Socialistic-type policies that promote a "spread the wealth" mentality only disincentivize people. It's been proven time and time again. The moment an individual realizes that their work is meaningless is the moment they stop caring and trying. And the moment society stops caring and trying is the moment our economy crashes.

There are certainly ways to provide *opportunities* for those who find themselves in difficult situations. There are ways to offer a hand so that people with less have a better chance to pull *themselves* up and build a successful future. I'm all for that. But we cannot allow emotion, guilt, and empathy to cloud our judgment and cause us to make wide-scale decisions that will jeopardize our economy.

REMOVE POLITICS

We won't spend much time at this stop because we've gone over it several times already. As I have said in other sections, it is incredibly important that every individual take time to self-educate and think independently. Just because you agree with one political figure or party on a couple of issues doesn't mean you should assume to agree with them on forty-seven other issues.

In many ways, political parties have become very similar to religion. Someone joins the Catholic faith, adopts Catholic beliefs as their own, and then orders their life accordingly. Same with politics. People assume that because they align with a political party on two to three issues, they should automatically assume to align on all issues. The fact that you are pro-LGBTQ rights shouldn't cause you to automatically assume that you are going to align with one particular party's position on the economy. And my strong feelings about gun laws shouldn't have any bearing on my beliefs about abortion. Think about each issue individually. Remove political bias. And for God's sake, *make up your own damn mind.*

MIND YOUR OWN FUCKING BUSINESS

At the root of many people's desire for increased regulations, rules, and systems lies a very powerful human emotion. And that is envy. Envy is defined as *"a feeling of discontented or resentful longing aroused by someone else's possessions, qualities, or luck."* This "resentful longing" gives way to anger and animosity toward those of generous means. It creates a negative stigma around being smart, wealthy, and successful. It promotes the idea that anyone who is successful is greedy and selfish. That they screwed someone over to get where they are at. That they are just lucky and were handed a golden ticket while everyone else lost out.

It wasn't always this way. Once, we prized success and highlighted achievement as a nation. Now we seem to martyr the victim and vilify the successful business owner. And here's what I would say to that...someone making ten million dollars probably has *nothing* to do with you. Unless someone broke into your bank account and funneled away your hard-earned cash, another person's success and wealth has no connection or correlation to yours. Again, there is no finite amount of money. *The person out there enjoying a nice slice of the American dream didn't steal your piece.* We're not all sharing one pie. You can go out and get your own slice, you can even make your own damn pie, and by all means, if you want to add some fucking ice cream to that, dream big and do it. But stop crucifying the hardworking individuals who were willing to do the things that you aren't to earn wealth and success.

People need to mind their own fucking business and spend their time and energy looking at their own lives and putting in the work to make something of themselves rather than blaming and resenting everyone else.

HOLD YOURSELF TO THE SAME OR HIGHER STANDARDS AS YOU HOLD EVERYONE ELSE TO

The last thing I would say before we jump into talking about solutions for some of our economic problems is this: across the board, our government spends way too much fucking money. This isn't just a problem with Democrats or a problem with Republicans. Both sides like to spend a fuck ton of money in different ways. Overspending is a problem for everyone. Both sides practice hypocrisy when it comes to how much they want at their disposal versus what they feel their opposition should be given. Both sides need to put away their pointing fingers and shut their open mouths ready to blame "the other side" for our economic problems. The amount of money that our government solicits from its people is just plain wrong. It needs to be reined in and cut back. It's going to require sacrifice and compromise, but *everyone* should be prepared to hold themselves to the same or higher standard as they hold others to.

With the blinders and biases removed, let's discuss strategies for improving and boosting our economy. Here are a few of my personal ideas and thoughts for solutions on the matter:

REMOVE AS MANY RESTRICTIONS AND REGULATIONS AS POSSIBLE

Other than an unforeseen disaster, the greatest danger our economy faces is us. It's the self-imposed restrictions, regulations, and governmental micromanaging that has the potential ultimately to stifle and kill what should be a booming economy.

To me, the more unfettered freedom we give to business owners to run their business as they see fit, the better. While the greatest danger our economy faces is over-restriction and overregulation, removing those same restrictions and regulations can create incredible stimulation and growth.

The only exception to this, and the one place where I do see it necessary for the government to provide some guidelines, pertains to monopolies and environmental issues.

Monopolies reduce the economic wealth of society in many ways, which is why it is beneficial for the government to regulate them with the objective of benefiting society. *Competitive firms* sell at market prices, which maximizes both consumer surplus and total surplus. In contrast, *monopolies* set prices to maximize their own profits, by decreasing supply and increasing their own producer surplus, which comes at the expense of both consumers and society. Ultimately, the economy produces less because of the monopoly. That's why having some regulations in place to prevent this from happening is beneficial for the health of our economy. These regulations help to prevent excess pricing, ensure quality of service, prevent the exploitation of monopsony buying power, and promote healthy competition. A great example of this was the 1984 case of the United States v. AT&T.

Environmental regulations and restrictions are also helpful, in some cases, for the well-being of our planet. Having said that, while there are certainly limits that should be set and standards that should be maintained, we're once again teetering over the line of overcorrection. The EPA demonstrates this very clearly. What began as an effort to set necessary and positive guidelines has now morphed into something so restrictive that we're beginning to create *a whole new problem.*

Obviously, regulations that keep companies from dumping toxic waste into a river should be in place. That's a no-brainer.

But if you have so many rules and restrictions in place that a company can't even operate, you've gone too far.

Though we talked about this in depth previously, I do want to note that imposed diversity hires also fit under the category of overregulation. In recent times, there has been a push to enforce quotas for diversity hiring within businesses. And while this may seem like a noble cause, it's a nasty and underhanded form of prejudice that promotes the idea that a particular group of individuals can't get certain jobs or succeed without special treatment. Not only does this kind of thinking create resentment, it is also detrimental to the progress we've made in abolishing negative prejudice in our society. Additionally, it stifles businesses' ability to make their own strategic decisions regarding the structure of their employees and organization.

All in all, regulations should be in place only when truly necessary. This is a perfect example of a time when less is absolutely more. Excessive restriction, regulation, and micromanagement will only lead to disincentivizing businesses. This can happen on a macro scale with large corporations and on a micro scale with individuals.

"But Mike, what about corrupt business owners? If there aren't rules and regulations on employers, good people are going to get screwed over."

Here's what I would say to that. Capitalism has a way of shaking out the bullshit. If you don't treat and pay your employees well, your services or product quality will suffer; which will, in turn, jeopardize your business. On the converse, if the government mandates that you pay employees a strenuously high rate, a business may be forced to cut their employee's hours back or send jobs to China just to stay in business.

When it gets down to it, businesses are only consumed by the bottom line. They revolve around making as much money as possible. And while this mentality may seem shrewd to some people or "the root of all evil," the fact of the matter is that our country has achieved the level of wealth and success it has largely because of the unfettered, capitalistic policies that allow for competition and freedom in business practices.

How many empires like Apple, Tesla, or Google, who have brought incredible technological innovation and advancement to the entire world, have come from communist countries? How many of the massive revolutionary concepts and products of the past several years were born in socialist societies? None of them. They've all come out of capitalistic environments—primarily from our country. Why? *Because capitalism breeds passion, incentive, and motivation, which in turn births new innovation and creation.*

Hamstringing and restricting this process through heavy governmental regulation will only drain us of the lifeblood of incentive and determination.

SET A FLAT TAX

Another thing that would greatly simplify our money process is to establish and implement a flat tax. Our existing process for calculating taxes is so confusing and filled with loopholes that it's become a game to see who can outsmart the system or pay someone enough to outsmart the system for them. This invites corrupt or shady business practices as people attempt to game the system for their benefit. With these dynamics in play, there will always be people who complain that "someone isn't paying enough" and that it's not fair that they have so much money.

A flat tax would fix all of this.

To me, a 10 percent tax across the board is easy and reasonable. It's an amount that just about anyone can get behind. To help those with lower income, I'd suggest that any individual who makes less than the collective mean average income (which could be easily calculated), should pay 5 percent. This ensures that everyone has skin in the game, is contributing, and doing their part. Whether you make $80,000 a year or $8 million a year, you would give 10 percent of it to taxes. No write-offs, no funny business, no getting around it. And you know what, I would bet you anything that a rigid, consistent standard like this would actually generate *more* money paid than what is "required" through our current shady, bullshit, "30ish-percent-before-write-offs-and-a-series-of-tax-code-gymnastic-tricks."

"But Mike, you don't understand. That won't pay for all the programs that our nation needs to fund. It's simply not enough money."

My response? Get rid of the fucking programs. Prioritize the ones that need to stay and get rid of the rest. You could also allow states to tax certain purchasable items to generate additional revenue from the people in a particular area to help pay for a particular program. But requiring people to pay increasingly more taxes is not the solution. It either *disincentivizes* people to chase success or incentivizes them to cheat or practice shady habits to get around the government's unreasonable, complicated demands. A flat tax system is un-cheatable. It's unbending, unchanging, and unbiased. Suddenly, the motivation for having offshore accounts, overseas factories, or hiring people for the sole purpose of getting out of paying taxes would be nullified. Businesses would be forced into the light with nowhere to hide. As a result, you'd also see a reduction in the resentment and negative stigma that surrounds people with wealth. When everyone is paying their share across the board, no one can look at someone else and accuse them of not doing their part or pulling their weight.

CUT BACK ON SPENDING ACROSS THE BOARD

Our nation spends far too much fucking money. And if we want to fix the money issues in our nation, we're going to have to change that. One of the first places we can cut back is foreign aid. I don't think a single cent of the American taxpayers' dollars should be spent on foreign aid without it being a stand-alone piece of legislation that is voted on in the House, then the Senate, and signed off on by the president. This entire process should be repeated each and every time we want to provide foreign aid to another country. There should be nothing attached to it, no earmarked aid bill for our own people, no tacking on funding for the post office or some governmental program. It has to be a stand-alone bill that everyone votes on. This helps to ensure that politicians are held accountable for their constituents' money that is being spent. It forces them to answer to the very people who put them into office for their decisions. It also ensures that if the collective decision is to send $12 billion to Iran, that decision has been made purely for the sake of sending $12 billion to Iran, not because of a domestic social program that got tacked onto it. This would eliminate massive amounts of excess spending that I consider to be waste, fraud, and an abuse of the system.

In general, I think that foreign aid could be cut back considerably. I would also propose pressing the pause button on foreign aid for four to five years and reallocating those funds into the US education system where the money would do much more good.

I would also propose putting a stop to the practice of subsidizing colleges. Colleges are a business like any other and shouldn't get any special breaks. Same for the NFL. And frankly, churches for that matter. I don't think churches should be tax free. There is an incredible amount of money that flows through them and if *any* group in our country should be the first to raise their hands and be willing to contribute to the betterment of our society, it should be those who belong to religious entities. One look at some of the shiny megachurches that line our city streets and it's obvious that there is a significant amount of money that funnels through the business of the church system. "Doing God's work" is supposed to be an act of helping people, not asking for a tax break so you can sit in a pew and listen to an inspiring speaker once a week. Please don't misunderstand me. I don't think there is anything wrong with churches and those who gain personal benefit from the programs they offer. But I don't think that churches should receive special treatment simply because they are a church. They should be taxed 10 percent just like everyone else.

In addition to these specific cutbacks that I've brought up, I think we need to significantly decrease general spending across the board. There are countless holes in our budget that constantly drain our resources. Campaign finance is one of these. As I proposed in a previous chapter, this could be eliminated if our election process was conducted in much the same way that certain counties choose grand juries: by serving papers and requiring the person who the most people nominated to fulfill their civic duty and serve their country. Again, this would completely abolish campaign finance corruption because there wouldn't be any campaigns, lobbyists, backhand deals to secure campaign financing, or wasting thousands of dollars to win the popularity contest. The only money spent in this situation would be exclusively on providing qualified individuals with a platform to share their ideas untouched by outside agendas and greedy entities that would seek to influence the election for their gain.

It's time to bring out the scissors and do some serious trimming. In a lot of areas. Everyone will have to make compromises. Everyone will have to make cutbacks. But it's the only way to see continued economic health and well-being.

In closing, I'd like to leave you with one actionable thing you can do that has immense power to generate positive change. And that is this: *Don't ever settle for identifying as a victim.*

Go out there and prove to yourself, your family, your city, your state, and your country that you are a productive member of society. Go out there and prove anyone who ever doubted you or misjudged you wrong. If everyone in our country took it upon themselves to stop making excuses and instead seized every opportunity given to them, we'd see positive change surge through our nation with such power that we wouldn't even know what to do with ourselves.

There is no shortage of opportunity in this country. So get out there and do it. Put in the work and make the sacrifices. Reach for something big. Earn your success rather than demanding to be entitled to it. And at the end of the day, when your head hits the pillow and you close your eyes and take in a deep breath and reflect on your success, you'll know that every cent you've earned and every success you've achieved was by the work of your own two hands.

And few things in life compare to that feeling.

CHAPTER 13

*

FOREIGN POLICY

The last major issue that I'd like to discuss is United States foreign policy. Under this heading you have trade, diplomacy, sanctions, military/defense, intelligence, foreign aid, and global environmental policy. With these subjects come many considerations.

Should there be global environmental policies in place?

How will we know when it's time to send our military to foreign soil?

What about foreign aid and trade?

Just like economics, this topic seems shrouded in complicated jargon and complexity to most people. And understandably so. The entire need for establishing foreign policies in the first place is based upon the fact that there are numerous countries with a vast array of differing views on government, society, and culture that must all coexist together on planet Earth. Each country has its own unique culture, military capabilities, and set of geographical challenges or advantages. Each country also has its own self-interests and agendas that inform decisions made regarding resources, trade, oil and gas, etc. All of these things are factors that contribute to foreign policy.

Yet despite how intricate these issues are, more often than not, the most complicated problems require the simplest solutions. Especially in relation to our *perspective* on these issues. As always, we'll break this down using our four principles first and then I'll offer some of my personal thoughts and ideas on a few key foreign policy issues.

REMOVE EMOTIONS

With all the issues we've discussed so far, we've talked about the need to remove emotion from the equation before decisions are made and policies are created. This could not be more necessary when approaching foreign policy. Emotions such as rage, offense, and even intense human compassion *must* be laid aside when assessing major decisions on behalf of our nation. The international arena is not the time and place to make spontaneous decisions, experiment, and hope for the best. It requires rational minds, logical thinking, and measured action.

REMOVE POLITICS

I've said it before, but I'll reiterate it here because I think it's definitely worth noting again. *Just because you dislike or oppose a*

current president should not inform your beliefs around their deci-
sions regarding foreign policy. Don't automatically default to disagreement simply because you didn't vote for them. This goes
for both sides. Have the brains and balls to remove your political biases and think logically about each situation and issue.

There were many decisions that Obama made during his
presidency regarding the military that I thought were outstand-
ing such as his choice to give the United States unfettered autonomy and flexibility to utilize drone strikes in military operations.
He also authorized what I'll refer to as "assassinations" that
were necessary and called for. Though I'm sure there is other
more delicate and accepted terminology for these "incidents,"
they boil down to the United States strategically taking out leaders of terrorist organizations. And I think Obama made the fucking right call to give the green light. There are other decisions
that he made that I think were fucking terrible. Choices that
destroyed funding and troop morale. Choices that allowed for
social gender experiments to take place in the military, compli-
cating the decision-making process that should be, and has been,
based on the answer to a singular question: *"Does this make us a*
better fighting force?"

The same is true for the Trump administration and decisions
he made during his presidency. I agree with some and disagree
with others. To me, this should be expected—to support some
choices and dislike others. If you support or oppose 100 percent
of a president's decisions 100 percent of the time, you've got
to take a hard look and ask yourself if you're operating out of
preconceived biases.

I also find it wrong that conservatives crucified Obama for certain choices and then turned around and suddenly commended them when it was Trump who made the call years later. And vice versa. It's total bullshit. Nothing sows the seeds of resentment more than practicing hypocrisy in this way. I know I sound like a broken record at this point, but it is vital that all of us lay aside political bias as well as our likes or dislikes in regard to the person who's in the White House before we approach any issue—especially ones that are as important and weighty as foreign policy.

In the same vein of removing politics, I think it's important that leaders recruit subject matter experts and individuals with a proven track record to make decisions in regard to specific issues. If global environmental issues are on the table, bring in environmental experts. If it's time to go to war, bring in the motherfuckers who know how to win a war. Politicians should not be the only ones placed in a position of power to inform decision-making.

The last thing I'll say here is this: There was a time when our love for our country came first. There was a time when people knew how to lay aside their political differences, rally, and unify as a nation when things got rough. But sadly, it's not that way anymore. And that's a huge problem. We *must* learn to place our country's safety and well-being above our own political rifts and disagreements.

MIND YOUR OWN FUCKING BUSINESS

As Americans, we have a way of life that we enjoy. We have a certain standard of living that we want to maintain and a level of relative safety that we want to preserve on our piece of planet Earth for as long as possible. Here's the thing. If we want to sustain this way of life, we must also continue to collaborate with other nations to procure the resources required for our standards of modern living. We must also continually assess dangers that would threaten it.

When potential threats do arise, we are faced with the dilemma of whether or not to take action. We are forced to ask ourselves tough questions.

Does this threat warrant military involvement?

How do we know when it's time to draw a line in the sand and take drastic action?

To answer these questions, we'll use our macro/micro test. I like to use the analogy of a bar fight.

Let's say you're an average guy walking down the street one night and you look through the window of your local pub and see a nasty bar fight going on inside. You have a decision to make. Do you step into the bar? Do you get involved? Do you join the fight?

This bar fight translates into toppling regimes, mass genocide, and geopolitical problems on a macro level. Instead of fists flying and shot glasses breaking, it's invasions of territories and erasing borders. But whether you're looking at this scenario on a macro level or a micro level, the first thing that you need to understand is that *the moment you decide to walk through those doors, you will create enemies.*

By simply showing up on the scene, you are knowingly putting yourself in danger and painting a target on your own back. Having

said that, depending on the situation, if you decide to keep walking and not do a damn thing about the fight, you may also create enemies. Sometimes you're faced with a "damned if you do,
damned if you don't" type of scenario. In most cases, minding
your own business and *not walking into that bar fight is the safer bet.*

This translates to the macro view as well. Most of the time,
we would do well to mind our own fucking business and let
other countries figure out their own goddamn problems instead
of sticking our nose where it doesn't belong and giving ourselves a black eye in the process.

However, there *are* three scenarios that call for getting
involved. We'll take the "micro view" first, going back to the guy
walking down the street and seeing a bar fight:

The first and most obvious reason to involve yourself is if
that "bar fight" gets so out of control that it's putting you at risk
for harm. Even if you were not a part of the original dispute that
created the fight, the moment it escalates to the point that it is
spilling out onto the streets, placing your well-being in jeopardy,
it's time to get involved.

The second scenario in which it is necessary to get involved
is if you look through those bar windows and witness an atrocity
taking place that is so unjust, so hideous, and so evil that you
know you'll be unable to live with yourself if you don't try to
stop it.

And third, if you notice a close family member or friend getting the absolute fuck beat out of them inside, you may feel it
necessary to provide them support—proving that you have their
back at all costs.

All three of these examples can be translated to a macro level as well. You don't have to fully understand the inner workings of every foreign policy issue to logically assess whether or not the United States should get involved in an international conflict. You can take the bar fight scenario and amplify it to a macro level and use it as the criteria for whether or not entering into a fight is necessary by asking:

1. Is this conflict an existential threat to the United States' safety or way of life?

2. Is this a situation in which an atrocity is taking place so great that we cannot live with ourselves if we do not get involved?

3. Does this involve a close ally? Is it absolutely necessary to have their back, no matter what the cost is to us as a nation?

If the answer is no to all of these questions, then the dilemma of whether or not to get involved is easy to answer. It's a hard no. We'd be far better off minding our own fucking business.

If the answer to the first criteria, *"Is this conflict an existential threat to the United States' safety or way of life?"* is yes, that yields a very clear course of action. When there is a threat to our safety or way of life, that danger must be taken very seriously. There may also be disputes that arise around *a resource* that is integral to our way of life—such as oil and gas. In those situations, it is important to exhaust solutions and strategies such as the use of tariffs, sanctions, and implementing diplomatic strategies *before* taking military action.

The second two sets of criteria, *"Is this a situation in which an atrocity is taking place so great that we cannot live with ourselves if we do not get involved?"* and *"Does this involve a close ally? Is it absolutely necessary to have their back, no matter what the cost is to us as a nation?"* are where things get a little gray. How do you pick and choose who and what is worth our involvement?

For starters, it is imperative to understand that if we go through those doors, fists flying, and join the proverbial bar fight on behalf of someone else, we may find ourselves in over our heads. We need to make sure that we don't end up as bad off as the ones we're trying to save because we weren't smart and strategic in our approach.

There is also the unfortunate truth that our world has many pockets of evil and injustice. Just as there is no way to stop every murder and rape in our country, there is no way that we can put a stop to every injustice in our world. There are genocide, tyrannical dictators, and brutality in many countries worldwide, and the United States simply cannot help them all without spreading ourselves so thin that we risk losing everything.

In my opinion, if there is conflict *within a nation's own borders,* whether that be a civil war or genocide, it is best to stay out of the situation and let them figure things out on their own. I do not think that is worth the lives of our own countrymen to intervene in the case of a foreign civil war or a country abusing its own people. Perhaps that makes me sound like a callous asshole, but

I truly believe that the moment we designate ourselves as the mediator and moral police of the world, we place ourselves in a never-ending bar fight that will eventually beat the fuck out of us.

There certainly may be a few situations in which everyone agrees and recognizes that there is an atrocity so great in a particular region that it requires action from other nations to put a stop to it. I believe that action in situations like these will be apparent to all if and when the time comes. *But they should be the exception, not the norm.*

If a conflict escalates beyond the borders of a particular country and begins to involve other countries and territories— gaining enough power to have the potential to be a significant threat to the United States, that also calls for getting involved. In our bar fight metaphor, this is when the fight spills out of the bar and onto the streets and moves dangerously close to your house—putting your safety or way of life at risk.

In all of these cases, getting involved and entering into a fight should be a last resort. It should be avoided at all costs. Every negotiation and mediation should be sought after to circumvent it, every strategy exhausted to avoid it. But if and when the time comes that military action is required, it should be *swift*, *relentless*, and *enacted with such force* that our enemies regret the day they dared to fuck with the United States of America.

On this point I like to reference William Tecumseh Sherman, an American soldier, businessman, educator, and author who served as a general in the Union Army during the American Civil War and received recognition over the years for his command of military strategy. In his words:

War is hell. You cannot qualify war in harsher terms than I will. War is cruelty, and you cannot refine it. Those who brought war into our country deserve all the curses and maledictions a people can pour out.

The brutality and horror that war brings with it is unavoidable. I have looked it in the eyes, I have been much closer to it than most and can attest to this fact. If it is necessary to enter into a fight, your primary goal should be to minimize your own casualties, loss, and despair. And the most effective way to do this is to *treat your adversary with such brutality that they quickly lose the desire even to fight anymore.* This approach has been proven over millennium to be the most effective approach to war. To quote Tecumseh Sherman again,

"Every attempt to make war easy and safe will result in humiliation and disaster." He also adds, "War is cruelty. There is no use trying to reform it. The crueler it is, the sooner it will be over."

War *must* be viewed this way. You cannot go into battle with any ounce of compassion or empathy for your opposition. It will only hinder your ability to keep your own people safe. Half-hearted, timid actions only result in lengthy, painful wars that incur far more losses than swift and brutal action. That's why every option for peaceful resolution must be exhausted before military action is taken.

When you take that deep breath and cross over the threshold into the realm of war, you better be ready to burn that motherfucker down. The gloves need to come off. Whatever means required to accomplish the goal of absolute victory should be implemented. Your goal should be to wipe your enemy off the face of the earth. Surrender, on their part, any time before that is a bonus that will simply make the process a little easier.

If in our micro scenario you *do* join in that bar fight and someone pulls a knife out and starts trying to kill you, that's not the time to be worried about hurting them too badly or abiding by some bullshit set of rules on how it's okay to fight and how it's not okay to fight. You need to knock him out and make him regret ever fucking with you in the first place. Anything short of swift, definitive, brutal response only makes you vulnerable and gives your adversary the opportunity to kill you. In our macro scenario, if we're going to send our men and women to war, we'd better be ready to provide them with the autonomy and capabilities to execute the task at hand.

World War II is a textbook example of this entire step-by-step process in terms of *when* we got involved in the proverbial "bar fight," *how* we got involved, *why* we got involved, and *what* we did once we got involved. We waited to enter into the fight until it was obvious that the ensuing chaos was a direct threat to our safety and continued way of life. And when we entered the fight, we came ready to do whatever was necessary to defeat the enemy, even if that meant dropping an atomic bomb and leveling entire cities. World War II is also a consummate example of the proper protocol in the aftermath of war. The United States *still* has a military presence in Germany as we speak, even decades later. If you have to sacrifice the kind of blood and resources that we did to end a conflict, you better damn well make sure it doesn't happen again.

The moral of the story is this: when it comes to international conflict, if at all possible, *mind your own fucking business*. Keep your nose out of other people's business. Let them figure out their own damn lives. But if you must enter the fight, be swift, be ruthless, and *fucking end it*.

HOLD YOURSELF TO THE SAME OR HIGHER STANDARD AS YOU HOLD EVERYONE ELSE TO

In this same vein, I think it's important that we, as a nation, hold ourselves to the same standards that we hold others to. If we don't want others fucking around in our business, we shouldn't fuck around in theirs unless it's absolutely necessary to our nation's safety.

The United States is guilty of overextending itself in resources, manpower, and global courtesy. We go places that we are not welcome or wanted in order to further our personal agendas. And it pisses people off. Sometimes to the point of creating a new conflict. Guess what? Not all countries want to be a democracy. Not all countries want an American air force base set up in their backyard. And how can we blame them? The truth is that we'd have a real problem if Russia decided to build an air force base in Mexico and equip it with fighter jets. And if Iran decided to park an aircraft carrier twenty-five miles off the coast of California, we'd be none too pleased. We *cannot* go around poking our nose in everyone else's business if we don't want them poking their nose in ours. We have to hold ourselves, as a nation, to the same standard as we hold other countries to.

As with all of these things, there are exceptions and special circumstances that may be a factor for consideration in certain scenarios. I'm not advocating a complete isolationist mentality. There is a happy medium between getting involved and keeping to ourselves. In any case, applying our four principles will go a long way in simplifying our approach to many foreign policy issues and I'd like to share a few thoughts on a handful of those.

INTERNATIONAL TRADE

I'm not a trade expert by any stretch of the imagination, but it doesn't take one to recognize the benefits of free trade. In my opinion, we should trade with anyone and everyone. And we should remove as many unnecessary regulations as we can to make that possible. There are certain trade situations that may call for a "strong arm" approach in order to make it clear to the rest of the world that they can't fuck over the United States. This approach may involve imposing tariffs in a strategic manner or threatening trade restrictions. Tariffs, trade restrictions, and embargoes are all tools that could be implemented to achieve a desired outcome without going to war. In the case of a conflict, all of these things should be utilized and exhausted thoroughly before military action is taken.

On this note, I will add that negotiations only work if the potential for war taking place is realistic. On a micro level, think of children: once a child knows that he won't be disciplined, he will no longer respect authority because he knows he doesn't have to. All the begging and attempted negotiations in the world won't fix that. He'll run circles around you and do what he damn well pleases. On a macro level, other countries are the exact same way. Our ability to negotiate hinges on the fact that everyone understands that if that negotiation fails, they will be going to war with the United States of America. And if we've earned a track record of taking swift and brutal action when pushed into a position of having to go to war, then our reputation should precede us—giving us a strong upper hand in all negotiations. So if you're of the opinion that our United States military gets too much money, I'd like to remind you that the moment other nations cease to recognize us as a threat is the moment we lose all power in the global game.

At the foundation of all international interaction should be the understanding that we are a powerful and dangerous nation. And while we wield that power and danger with incredible voluntary control, we are also unafraid to unleash it should the need arise.

In the words of Jordan Peterson, "A harmless man is not a good man. A good man is a very dangerous man who has that under voluntary control."

FOREIGN AID

We covered this topic in the last chapter, but I feel that it's necessary to mention it here as well. I don't think any of the American taxpayers' dollars should be spent on foreign aid without it being a stand-alone piece of legislation and that nothing be attached to it. There should be no earmarked aid bill for our own people, no tacking on funding for social programs. Overall, it would also be wise to make drastic cutbacks on the amounts we give and reinvest those funds into our own nation's well-being and our future generations.

GLOBAL ENVIRONMENTAL POLICY

The last thing I will touch on here is global environmental policy along with overall environmental issues since we have yet to discuss these topics.

Let's start by talking about overall environmental issues. This is a classic example of a subject that's been assaulted by political bias and high emotions. You've got this side screaming one thing and the other side screaming the complete opposite. As with most things, the answer usually lies somewhere in the middle. So here's my take on it: Do I think the world is going to end in twelve years due to environmental changes? No, I do not. But do I think humans have a negative impact on the planet and should do a better job caring for it? Absolutely. Things like biodiversity, water pollution, deforestation, and climate change are serious issues that deserve to be discussed and researched and I think we, as a human race, need to do a far better job caring for this planet that we live on. I'm not an environmental expert and don't have to be to come to this logical conclusion.

If you can be dead by starting a vehicle in your garage in a matter of minutes from the emissions, it is not a quantum leap to assume that those same emissions will have some impact on our environment. As will dumping oil in our rivers or cutting down every fucking tree on the planet. I also think that population size has a major impact on the environment. It's an uncomfortable subject, because there aren't many great solutions for it, but it needs to be at least acknowledged and discussed.

Having said that, I also think that there is a lot of misinformation out there about climate change and other environmental issues. These "facts" are often presented in a way that is designed to incite fear, further political agenda, and stir up strife. As individuals, we should do our own research, assess credible data, look to trusted sources, and listen to experienced scientists and subject matter experts. Subject matter experts and proven scientific data should be the greatest influencers of decisions made regarding the environment, especially when it comes to large-scale decisions. This is definitely true when it comes to proper care for our evergreen and seasonal forests, oceans, and rainforests.

Just as a politician who's never shot a gun before has no business leading troops into battle, politicians who exist within an air-conditioned bubble and rarely venture into the woods should not be the ones tasked with making major decisions regarding our forests. Some experts have dedicated their entire lives to the intricacies of the forest, the fine details of climate change and pollution, and every imaginable environmental issue. These experts should be placed in positions of power and then we, as a nation, need to sit our collective ass down and fucking listen to what they have to say. And then we need follow it—without inserting a political agenda.

As far as *global* environmental policy goes, I do think that our environment deserves international collaboration and teamwork to keep our planet healthy, both for our own benefit and the benefit of generations to come. However, there will be countries that don't give a fuck about our collaborative efforts and will continue to do whatever the hell they want in terms of the environment.

Sure, we could use tariffs and sanctions and refuse to trade with them in an effort to force them into submission on the issue, but there's no guarantee that those strategies will even work. And if they don't, we've got a choice to make. Is this environmental policy worth going to war over? I'm not going to say that they are or aren't worth going to war over—I would leave that to scientists and trusted data that assess the risks and dangers before determining that. But I do think it's a very necessary consideration that must be entered into the equation when approaching global policy.

In closing, as always, I'll leave you with two things you can do as an individual in regard to this issue:

STAY IN YOUR LANE

One of the most important things you can do is to know when something is outside your wheelhouse and how to stay in your own lane. If you've never served in the military, don't pretend to be an expert on how a military should conduct themselves. There are far too many self-appointed experts shouting their opinions to the masses that have no idea what the fuck they are talking about. It only muddies the water and creates more division and confusion. Know when it's time to trust an expert on a particular subject and don't open your mouth unless you know what you're talking about. And stop second-guessing every decision made and action taken simply because you don't like the guy in the White House who signed off on it.

LEARN THE STORY OF THE WORLD

The final thing I will leave you with is this. *Educate yourself and your children on world history.* I cannot overstate this. Don't be naive and ignorant to the lessons that the human race has learned countless times over throughout the previous millennia. There is absolutely no excuse for this level of ignorance when we have so many books and educational tools at our fingertips. Don't just send your children to public school and call it a day. Find books from various time periods and places around the world and read them all. Let the variety round out your perspectives and give you a full and accurate view of history. Read about the Roman Empire, the Mongols, the Persian Empire, and the Ming Dynasties. Give yourself the benefit of understanding how we, as humans, arrived at where we are in this day and time. Don't settle for being spoon-fed or staying in the dark.

If we hope to succeed as a nation and as a collective species, we have to understand where we have come from. We must comprehend and harness the wisdom passed down to us by the lives, victories, and mistakes of those who have gone before us.

Only stupidity would cause us to reap the painful harvest of avoidable mistakes simply because we are too lazy to learn the lessons that history so generously offers us.

CHAPTER 14

★

YOU

Well, my friend, the time has come to wrap this conversation up. Not that there's not more that we could discuss. There always is. But we'll save it for another time. If we were in my living room or on my back porch we'd take the last swig of our beer and throw down some barbecue. That feels like the only proper ending to a good discussion like this.

So far I've done the majority of the talking here, due to the format of written words in which I've chosen to share my thoughts. But, just as I said at the start of this book, this is the beginning of a conversation. This is a two-way street. I'd love to hear your thoughts on the topics we've discussed here. While I can't promise that I will be able to respond to each and every email or DM, I will certainly do my best to respond as often as I can.

But even more than a conversation between you and me, I hope this book will spark a conversation between you and others. I hope it ignites thoughtful, productive conversations between you and the people that you love, work with, and play with. Maybe even with those you don't love or like much at all. I hope that this book is a tool to help you peel away the web of political biases, sensitivities, emotions, social expectations, and conditioning that surrounds the important topics of our day. I hope that we can all stop contorting and tiptoeing because we're so afraid of setting off some offensive alarm. I hope that after you shut these pages you'll have the courage to clear your throat and start honest, kind, face-to-face conversations around kitchen tables and bar counters, in backyards, cafés, or hell, even titty bars. I hope it sparks new thoughts and ideas, new perspectives and broadened views. I hope you do it through laughter and with as many inappropriate jokes as you can muster.

Because I don't want the conversation to stop with you and me. I have a limited perspective and so do you. We need our thinking expanded, challenged, and sharpened by other great minds. We need more conversations about important issues that aren't surrounded by a minefield of potential offense. We need to bring back the art of face-to-face conversation, filled with thoughtful speaking and thoughtful listening. With smiles and laughs and slaps on the back over good food and drink or in the great outdoors.

It is my hope that you see this book as an invitation to do just that.

Before we call it a day, I want to finish this talk where all conversations of this nature should. I want to end by talking about you and me and what we can do when we wake up tomorrow to move the needle of our world in the right direction, no matter how slightly. All the discussions and debates in the world aren't worth shit if individuals don't take responsibility for their lives and turn talk into action. Only when enough individuals rise up and start taking action in their sphere of life will we see a collective tidal wave that shifts and changes society.

And that begins with us.

We've discussed a lot of weighty topics—from challenges in our economy to human trafficking to drug trade to border security to social issues. These are heavy topics and challenges. They are big, they are complex, and at times, they are seemingly insurmountable to overcome. It's easy to feel like you and I don't have anything to contribute, any way to help create a shift in our society and world at large.

That's why I want to end this book by sharing with you a handful of things that you can put into practice *immediately* in your own life. All of these are things that I strive to practice in my own life. They are things that I have seen proven time and again to have a positive impact both in the lives of individuals as well as society at large. I'm by no means perfect or feel that I have arrived on any of these points. But you can bet your ass that I wake up every day doing what I can to progress, learn, and grow.

SHIFT YOUR MENTALITY

In many ways, this book has been all about shifting mentality and perspective. The word mentality is defined as *"the characteristic attitude of mind or way of thinking of a person or group.*" All of us should make it our mission to pursue independent and informed thinking, to check and recheck our mentality about ourselves and the world around us constantly. It is a journey that each of us will be on for life. There are two mental shifts that I believe can do the most good in your life as an individual and society at large.

1. Think for Yourself

The idea of thinking for yourself has been a theme throughout this entire book. And that is intentional. As we have discussed, we all must be aware that we are constantly inundated with a barrage of powerful forces that seek to influence the way we think. If we don't fight for independent thought, if we allow ourselves to go on autopilot, we will fall into that dangerous herd mentality—dumbly following the strongest influence and loudest voice without question. And that's when things get scary. When you have an entire society that pliable and that moldable, bad things happen. I'm talking sci-fi, brainwashed humanity, susceptible to evil kinds of scary shit. Yet we're the ones doing it to ourselves.

So think independently. Think for yourself. Break free from the boxes that this world tries to put you in and labels they try to put on you. Don't let the fact that you're a woman, an urbanite, a person of color, or a Baptist who lives deep in the South automatically cause you to make assumptions about how you should think, feel, or vote on any issue. Stop letting the country, the media, society, or anything else tell you how you're supposed to feel or think. You are unique. And your thoughts and beliefs, your opinions and convictions should be too. So when you begin to look at or assess any subject, be hypervigilant to remove politics, emotions, preconceived notions, biases, and societal conditioning. We need your independent mind. We need your thoughts, solutions, and strategies in their purest form.

If every individual would make this one simple mentality shift, we would see wild, inconceivable change take place. The days of identity politics, rampant division, divisiveness, and herd mentality would be long gone. You'd see the lines between what it means to be a Republican or a Democrat gray as individuals refuse to be painted with a broad brush or told how to think. The lines between political parties and camps would melt and blur, giving way to the melding of great minds and free thinkers who will bring forth the solutions, innovations, and creativity that we need to stand up to our challenges.

This one mentality shift is something that you can begin pursuing *right now*. Start asking questions. Starting thinking for yourself, educating yourself, researching for yourself. Expose yourself to a variety of deep thinkers, innovators, philosophers, political leaders, experts, and friends who think both similarly and differently than you.

And don't stop there. Turn those well-informed thoughts, beliefs, and opinions into action by exercising your right as an American citizen to vote. Don't vote for the lesser of two evils, don't vote for the one person who's just "not the other guy." Would you choose a spouse simply because they are not as bad as your ex? Fuck, I hope not. No one goes around making important choices with a shrug and a "I-guess-it's-the-lesser-of-two-evils" kind of mentality. So don't adopt that kind of thinking when it comes to who is leading our nation and impacting the future of the next generation. Think and research for yourself. Draw your own beliefs and conclusions. And then vote according to those beliefs; vote for the absolute best person for the job.

2. Take Responsibility

No matter who you are or what stage of life you are currently in, it's important to remember that *someone* is looking at you. You are an example *to* someone and you are an influence *on* someone. That alone should be a weighty responsibility. It's one that none of us should take lightly. Take responsibility and ownership for what is yours. Don't blame your problems on other people; put your head down and own the shit that's yours to own. If you make a mistake, don't pretend that you didn't. Don't try to cover it up. Look it square in the face, own it, and take action to grow from it. In doing so, you'll show others that it's okay to fall down and get back up.

Nobody, and I mean fucking *nobody*, likes a finger pointer. Have you ever sympathized with someone who blamed someone else for their mistakes and problems? Fuck no. No one earns respect by pointing fingers and blaming others for their problems. So stand up and own what's yours to own. Take responsibility for your thoughts, actions, and the example you're setting for those who are watching.

Mark my words, if everyone adopted these two mentality shifts, our society would change drastically.

MASTER THE TRIFECTA OF HEALTH

We've spent a good portion of this book talking about your mental space—your thoughts, perspectives, influences, and everything that goes on between your ears. But I don't want to stop there. To me it is *vital* to take ownership of your body as well as your mind. In many ways they are inextricably linked, the mind and body. Once you begin to take ownership of your body, you will find yourself taking ownership of your mind and thoughts. And, when you begin taking ownership of your mind and thoughts, you will find yourself taking ownership of your body.

Our physical health impacts our mental health. It affects our clarity of thought, susceptibility to disease, productivity, and quality of life. It affects everything. Throughout several parts of this book we've discussed the crisis of health in our nation and the impact it has, not only on individuals but on our healthcare system and national finances.

It doesn't take much research to see that the American food system is pretty fucked-up. We've modified foods that didn't need to be modified and we've created foods that are full of artificial ingredients. We've also created such an optimized lifestyle that we spend the better part of our lives sitting in climate-controlled, artificially lit rooms without taking more than a few steps each day.

This isn't a little problem, it's a big problem. Flip back and look at some of the startling statistics that we've covered in previous chapters and it's evident that something has to change. And that comes down to you and me. It comes down to individuals taking control of their own goddamn piece of humanity and making choices to care for it.

The good news is that there *is* a solution. A very simple one, in fact. It's not some mind-blowing silver bullet. And while it may be *simple*, that doesn't mean that it's *easy*. The solution lies in applying common-sense ideas *consistently*. It's straightforward but pretty damn effective.

So don't fall for the fads and gimmicks that constantly confuse the conversations on health, wellness, and fitness. *If something sounds too good to be true, it probably is.* Despite what the media and advertisements scream, you don't need some thirty-day challenge or crazy cleanse or five-day boot camp or weight loss drug. You don't need to be extreme or fanatical. You need to nail the basics and be as consistent as you can in doing so.

There is a wealth of information out there on all things health, nutrition, and fitness. I would encourage you to read, research, and educate yourself on these subjects. But don't get overwhelmed. When you boil it all down, there are three primary things to aim for to maintain a solid baseline of health. I like to call it the *Trifecta of Health*.

1. Get the Fuck Outside
2. Get Off Your Ass
3. Get Proper Fuel

Simple? Yes. Easy? Not always. To be a healthy individual, you need *all three* of these. You can't just nail one and forget the other two or nail two and forget the other one. Let's break them down:

GET THE FUCK OUTSIDE

Guess what? You are an animal. And animals are meant to be outside. Humans like to think of themselves as "oh so special," but we are a species on this earth like any other. And that means that we need to spend time in the great outdoors in order to be healthy. There are numerous studies and proven science to back this up.

You need sunlight. You need fresh oxygen. You need to spend at least a portion of your time in environments that are natural. Human beings are natural and should spend time in natural environments. This is important for *disconnection* as well as *sustenance*. You need *disconnection* from blinking lights, screens, information flow, and numerous other things that create the artificial bubbles we spend most of our days in. You also need *sustenance* through sunlight and oxygen to nourish your body and mind.

There is also an element of grounding that happens when we place ourselves in natural environments. We reconnect with what is real. We gain perspective on what matters and what doesn't. Getting the fuck outside is something we should do every day. Additionally, I think that every human being would benefit from an extended period of exposure to the outdoors for several days at least a few times per year. Away from the mundane hamster wheel of routine, away from technology, away from the comforts and artificially controlled environments we exist within day to day, our minds have a chance to clear. To quiet. To be fully present. Watch and be observant and you will see your perspective change.

Your mind will shift as your sole focus becomes purifying your water, gathering firewood, building your shelter, watching for when the sun rises and sets, and observing shifts in the weather. Your mind becomes present and wholly consumed with attending to the most basic elements of your human needs. It's a beautiful thing, really. It takes your mind off of all the tiny stressors and stimuli that constantly assault you. It gives you perspective as to what matters and doesn't. It renews your sense of gratitude for the comforts you've been afforded. It decreases depression and increases well-being. It's cleansing. It's relaxing. It's cathartic.

And it's necessary.

So get the fuck outside.

GET PROPER FUEL

There is more accessible information about nutrition now than there ever has been. This also means that you can find experts who back completely conflicting dietary theories. You can find "research" and "clinical studies" for one diet and the same "proof" for a completely opposing dietary approach. It seems that with each passing year, information increases while overall health decreases. Eating and properly fueling your body shouldn't be that complicated.

So let's make this simple.

Imagine your body is a car for a minute. If you put shitty fuel in the tank, what's going to happen? It's going to run shitty. It's going to fuck up the engine. It's going to affect the car's ability to get where it needs to go efficiently. The same is true of you. You can't put shitty food in your body and expect to think clearly, have energy, be productive, sleep well, and live a long, high-quality life.

Unfortunately, there's a lot of shitty fuel out there. There are many foods in the standard American diet that are just plain poisonous. Foods that are screwing up our lives, fucking up our minds, negatively impacting our children, and doing much more damage than most people realize or are aware of.

So start by educating yourself. Give enough of a shit about your health to take time to empower yourself on how to fuel your body properly. Don't get caught in the web of fads and conflicting information. Apply the KISS principle here, i.e., *Keep It Simple, Stupid.*

If you boil down all the hype and bullshit, you can sum up good nutrition practices into these five common-sense habits:

1. Eat lean, high-quality protein. If your protein source comes from an animal, make sure you're aware of what *they ate* while alive. If the animal ate shitty fuel and then you eat the animal, you're taking in the shitty fuel. Spend the extra money for quality protein; it's worth it.

2. Eat generous amounts of fresh vegetables, a little bit of fruit, and some healthy fats through sources like nuts and seeds.

3. Cut out sugar entirely, except for special occasions. Not only cookies, cake, and ice cream but also sugar-laden processed foods and drinks.

4. Limit starchy, flour-based, artificial products, and
    processed carbohydrates as much as possible. This
    includes things like crackers, cookies, pasta, granola
    bars, tortillas, bread, muffins, chips, etc. While there are
    certainly some of these items on the market that are
    made with high-quality ingredients, the majority of foods
    in this category are low-quality and full of things that
    are anything but healthy. Don't assume that everything
    labeled, "contains whole grains" is actually a quality food.
    If you are going to eat grains, choose an actual whole
    grain. That means that you should be able to *see the whole
    grain* on your plate. Think rice, whole oats, and quinoa.

5. And lastly, drink mostly water. Do away with sodas,
    sweet cocktails, and your salted-caramel-pumpkin-
    spice-fucking-whipped-cream-topped bullshit excuse
    for coffee.

Eat this way for the majority of the time and then allow yourself room to eat things you enjoy a few times a week that may
not fit within these guidelines. It's okay to have a few beers or
a glass of wine every now and then. You can have your fajitas
or pizza night with the family every once in a while. Aim for
creating habits that are sustainable and something that you can
maintain with consistency. You don't have to be uptight and you
don't have to be perfect. You don't need to be on a diet. You
don't need a quick fix or multilevel marketing scheme to keep
you on track. You just need *consistency*.

Keep in mind that even with just the foods I mentioned above, there are countless ways to make healthy versions of all of your favorite dishes. There are ways to effectively flavor, season, and prepare meals that you can truly enjoy eating. It's worth taking the time to discover healthy food preparations and dishes that you'll look forward to eating, that you'll savor and enjoy. No one will remain consistent in eating foods that they can't stand. You don't have to eat a reheated, frozen chicken breast and unseasoned, limp broccoli. Learn how to make your food taste good and remember that your taste buds will also change and adapt more quickly than you think. Your taste buds may be desensitized from an excess of salt, sugar, and fat and that may make it hard to enjoy the subtle, wholesome flavors of real food at first. But again, that will quickly change.

Think of the kid who turns his nose up at a beautifully aged piece of cheese because he's expecting processed squirt cheese from a can or asks for a Hot Pocket instead of finishing his perfectly seared Wagyu rib eye. His taste buds just haven't learned to appreciate quality yet. Give it time and soon you'll find yourself actually *preferring* the flavors of whole food over all the processed shit. And remember that just because something is convenient doesn't mean it's the right choice.

In addition to choosing quality foods, I also think it's important to pay attention to how you consume them. The setting and manner in which you eat matter. We live in a society where technology and mass production of agriculture and farming has removed us from the process of growing, harvesting, butchering, gathering, and preparing food. Humans are disconnected from food in a way that they have historically never been. And that has a negative impact on our health. People aren't aware of where their food comes from or what's in it. Food has become merely an item. It's no longer a part of culture, family, and lifestyle.

For centuries people have spent a significant amount of their time growing their food, preparing it, talking about it, and gathering around to eat it. They invested their effort and heart into the process. When they bit into a juicy tomato or relished the first strawberry of the season, they remembered the tiny seeds they planted, the hours tending the fields in the sun, the careful way they watched over the plants. When they salted and seared a steak over flame, they knew the months of care it took to raise that cow and the work invested in butchering and preserving the meat. This understanding, this connection to food and the process of bringing it to the table, brings forth gratitude. It brings thankfulness, mindfulness, and a sense of being present. It brings forth the desire to share the fruits of your labor with people you love.

I'm not saying that you need to buy a farm or butcher a cow. But it is important to take time to sit, eat slowly, savor your food, think about where it came from, and be grateful for the journey it took to arrive on your plate. I know this may sound like some kind of hocus-pocus, hippie shit, but it's not. It's in us; it's primal. It's part of human history. And it's an important part of eating well.

Nutrition is not the only type of fuel your body needs. It also needs quality sleep and the absence of chronic stress. There are countless studies that show the detrimental effects of inadequate sleep and chronic stress. Some studies have even gone so far as to prove that the symptoms of being acutely sleep-deprived are often worse than being drunk. Being chronically sleep-deprived affects your adrenals, central nervous system, brain, and insulin resistance.

You can have everything else dialed in, from your nutrition to your exercise regime, but it will affect everything if your sleep is off. Humans need rest to function well. That means going to bed at a reasonable hour, at least a few hours before midnight, and sleeping at least seven and a half hours. And that sleep needs to be high quality. Invest in a good pillow and blackout shades. Keep the house quiet and turn the TV and other devices off. It doesn't have to be perfect, just do the best you can with what you have and you'll notice a significant impact in the way you feel, your productivity, and overall health.

It's also important to keep an eye on your stress levels. Ongoing, chronic stress is not good for the body. It sets off a whole chain reaction that makes everything more difficult—from making good food choices to getting good sleep. If you can't control, affect, or change something, let it go and don't spend your mental energy stressing over it. I know that's easier said than done and I find myself falling short on this far too often. Again, simply do your best and be mindful of it and you're already ahead of the game.

GET OFF YOUR ASS

The last aspect of our Trifecta of Health is exercise and moving your body. I could include studies and statistics out the ass about why it's vital to good health, but I think most people are already aware of its importance. You have a body and you need to move it to maintain good health, lower stress levels, and avoid injury.

As with nutrition, there is an excess of information surrounding the simple act of exercising. When you boil it all down, the most important thing is that you move your body. That's something you can do anytime, anywhere. Walk to the store instead of driving, pick a parking spot that's farther away from the door, take the stairs, do some yard work. These are simple ways to get your body moving, things you can do all throughout your day. Again, apply the KISS principle. Anything is better than nothing. Just get off your ass.

If you'd like to be more intentional and strategic about moving your body in the form of organized workouts, go for it! There are incredible benefits to doing so. As far as the details on *what* that looks like, that is up to you. There is not one thing or one way for everyone to approach exercise. The goals of a sweet little ninety-year-old grandmother and a high school quarterback are going to be vastly different. *Your* goals should drive what your plan of action is. Do a little research and experimentation and then set some realistic and specific goals. Assess where you're at and where you want to go and then find people who can help guide you in the process of getting there. And if you don't find a goal that you want to work toward, pick a sport that involves some physical activity and get out there and fucking learn it or jog around your neighborhood. I want to add that there is such a thing as overtraining. Don't do it. That's just as unhealthy as undertraining. Give your body proper rest and recovery. Be smart, be sensible.

This Trifecta of Health can be likened to a three-legged stool. The stool cannot stand without each of its legs. You need all three aspects that we talked about here represented in some form or fashion in your life if you want good health. Again, it doesn't have to be perfect. It just needs to be consistent.

If you're sitting there reading this and you feel overwhelmed because you're overweight, you hate working out, you are addicted to ice cream, or you haven't gotten out of your office cubicle and into the sun in weeks, then you are probably thinking, *"Fuck, where do I even start?"* Don't panic. Just start somewhere. With every decision you make comes a fork in the road where you have the opportunity to ask yourself, *"Is this decision going to help me get one step closer to my goals or one step farther from my goals?"* It's a simple question, but if you let it guide 99 percent of the choices you make, it will have a profound impact on your life. There will be exceptions, mistakes, and deviations. And that's okay.

The important thing is to be specific about your goals, rather than making broad, generalized statements such as, "I'm going to try to do better, eat better, or be better." There is no way to quantify or define a goal like that and you'll crash before you even leave the runway. Spend some time digging deep and homing in on what exactly success in these areas means to you and then set doable, small steps to achieve it. Don't look at how far you have to go, look at what you can do in the next week, the next day, hell, even the next hour to get one step closer to your goals.

I realized very quickly in SEAL training that the guys who quit were the ones who became fixated on the fact that it was going to last for six months. They kept telling themselves over and over that it was going to be a six-month kick in the nuts and that there was no way they could last that long. And they didn't. The people who obsessed on how far they had to go were often the ones who quit. I learned that the only way to get through the rigorous and exhausting demands of SEAL training was to take it one step at a time. Even taking it a day at a time would have proven to be too overwhelming in some cases. I couldn't think about tomorrow or next week or next month. I couldn't think of how far I had to go. I just had to find it within me to take the next step.

This is something that can be applied in many areas in life and certainly to this conversation as well. If you are unhealthy, if you have a lot of weight to lose, if you have a lot of bad habits to break, set goals for where you want to go, and then focus on taking the next step. And then the next. And then the next.

FIND WAYS TO BE OF SERVICE

No matter who they are or what hand they've been dealt in life, everyone can do something to help or serve others. If we want to see a better future, a better country, a better society, or even a better version of ourselves, then each of us must dedicate a portion of our time to be of service to others or to be a part of something that is bigger than ourselves.

There is a sense of purpose that comes from helping other people that is incredibly positive and beneficial. Not only will you be able to help others, but you will also gain confidence, you'll feel grounded in a sense of purpose, and it will do absolute wonders for your mental health. And remember that you are an example to someone. Someone is looking at you, watching how you use your time. So be generous and do something for someone else; be part of something bigger than yourself.

I can't tell you *what* that will be because it should be different for everyone. It will be driven by the hundreds of intangibles that make you who you are. It may be joining the Peace Corps or military, doing community service, volunteering at the Boys and Girls Club, YMCA, or church youth group. There are hundreds if not thousands of possibilities of things you can do. Pick the one you're the most passionate about, the one that inspires you the most, or the one you feel will make the biggest impact in the world and then *go and do it*. What matters is that you do something bigger than you, something that is not about you, something that is for others.

You may think that you have nothing to offer, but *everyone*, and I mean everyone, can find some way to help their fellow man and make a positive impact on the world around them. And if we have more people willing to roll up their sleeves and get out there and help, we'd see a lot more solutions and a lot fewer problems in our world.

WRITE A PERSONAL CONSTITUTION AND LIVE BY IT

All of the things that we've talked about in this chapter are actionable choices you can make the moment you put this book down. *You alone* have the power to shift your mentality, to care for your body, to be of service. All the conversations and discussions in the world will not change society.

Change will only occur when enough individuals like you and I take action—starting with our own minds, bodies, and choices.

If you want to live a life that matters, that stands for something, and that makes a difference, you need to set an aim and purpose for your life. As with any goal or business plan, you have to have an idea of where you're going if you want to get there. And you can't be vague about it.

That's why it is my strong recommendation that you write up a personal constitution. Before you do this, I want you to take some time and give yourself a quiet space to think. Close your eyes for a moment and imagine a person who exemplifies everything you believe a person ought to be. Someone who is the pinnacle of a strong example that others can follow. Someone filled with integrity. Someone who is the embodiment of your principles, beliefs, and morals. Then think of all of the elements that made up and created that character. Be specific, be detailed. Use these elements as the foundation to write your personal constitution, a document that you can live by and base your life upon. Write down a list of those principles, ideals, and moral codes, and then use it as a guide to order your life by. For me, those principles are ones that I've threaded throughout this book and things I strive to live by every day. Yours will be different, and they should be. Your constitution should reflect your vision and values.

Don't just aim for "being better," aim with precision and strategy. Set personal metrics by which to measure whether or not you're achieving the things you've set out to achieve. When you get clear on your aim in life, you make it tangible when you pen it with ink. You make it something you can feel, touch, and hold in your hand. It solidifies your purpose. It turns hopes and desires into goals and action.

It's not a coincidence or accident that I call this a constitution. This nation was founded upon the bedrock principles of the United States Constitution. It's the basis of our laws and government. The word constitution is defined as *"a body of fundamental principles or established precedents according to which a state or other organization is acknowledged to be governed."* It's a powerful word attached to a powerful document. It has formed, shaped, and guided our nation.

So write a constitution of your own and strive to live by it. Let it govern your choices. Let it be a benchmark by which you can measure yourself. Let it be something you fall back on, that you are guided by, something that brings you back to center when you go off course and reminds you of what matters when you get distracted. Let it be your lighthouse, your compass.

Our country is facing a lot of challenges right now. And we need individuals like you to have the courage to think independently, to live with sincerity and integrity, and to roll up their sleeves and contribute to the world around us. We each have a part to play and a path to take that is, and should be, different from one another. There are times when you may feel like you're swimming upstream. You may feel insignificant or inconsequential in the grand scheme of life. But don't give up.

Because your life, that individual thread that you've been given to weave alongside countless others, is what will create the tapestry of the next chapter in history. What will be on that tapestry and what we will be remembered for...

...is up to us.

Or you could just forget this whole conversation ever happened.

In that case, go choke yourself.